LEAD, SERVE, WIN.

What it takes to build a mission-driven team from the ground up!

BY

TIM PRUNYI

LEAD, SERVE, WIN.

Copyright © 2022 by Tim Prunyi.

All rights reserved. No part of this publication may be reproduced, distributed, or transmitted in any form or by any means, including photocopying, recording, or other electronic or mechanical methods, without the prior written permission of the author, except in the case of brief quotations embodied in critical reviews and certain other non-commercial uses permitted by copyright law.

Ordering Information: Quantity sales. Special discounts are available on quantity purchases by corporations, associations, and others. Orders by U.S. trade bookstores and wholesalers.

www.DreamStartersPublishing.com

TIM PRUNYI

Table Of Contents

Foreword 4

Dedication 5

Introduction 7

Put God First 9

Progress, Not Perfection 20

You Will Be Hated 33

Your Body is a Temple 53

To Thine Own Self, Be True 69

Delegate the Details 77

Don't Delegate the Vision 92

Stand Up for Others 104

Speak Truth to Power 110

Believe In Yourself – Know Your Weaknesses 120

Support Your Team's Side Hustle 130

Let Your Yes Be Yes – Let Your No Be No 136

Conclusion 144

LEAD, SERVE, WIN.

Foreword

Tim Prunyi exemplifies servant leadership. He has dedicated his life to helping others. Whether showing veterans how to start their own businesses or working with orphans around the globe, Tim is happiest when he gets to help others achieve their dreams.

When I met Tim, he was finishing his MBA, and American Dream U was looking for someone to revitalize our MVP program for military veterans. He was the only person I spoke to who came with a concrete plan. Not only did he have a plan, but he had the enthusiasm to execute on it. We need more individuals who can execute. This is rare today

In this book, Tim shows you how to create your own plan to build the team of your dreams. Do you have what it takes to execute the mission?

Phil Randazo, Founder of American Dream U

Dedication

To Jon Thomas Banning, who started JTB Landscapers with an old chevy and a shovel, and now employs many dozens and helps many thousands;

To Phil Randazzo who founded American Dream U to help countless veterans follow their dreams and start their own businesses;

To Kim Sinatra - one of the top lawyers in the country - who taught me about treating your team right, and to talk the same way to the governor as to the housekeeper;

To Shaan Patel, founder of Shark Tank and Mark Cuban company Prep Expert, who taught me how to multitask;

To Clay Cooper, the most ethical man I know;.

To Alex Charfen, who taught me that entrepreneurs really are wired differently;

LEAD, SERVE, WIN.

To Pastors Jud Wilhite and Shawn Williams of Central Church, who taught me that God created our strengths to be used passionately and enthusiastically;

To Jeff Vowell, my scoutmaster who helped all of us struggle bus kids become Eagle Scouts;

And most importantly to my mom, who sacrificed everything so that my sister Stephanie and I could have everything she didn't.

Introduction

Building a team is like building a house; you need a blueprint of your final product, and you better lay your foundation before starting the roof.

The fact that teams are made of people makes this process infinitely more complex, but it doesn't have to be! You need to find that right fit, train them, and let them do their magic. At the end of each chapter, I will ask you to write. You don't need to get a special notebook just to read this book, but there is a certain magic that comes from putting pen to paper. By the end of this book, you will be equipped to create your dream team and accomplish your mission.

Are You My Tribe?

First of all, thank you for picking up this book. There are millions of show, movies, podcasts, and other books competing for your attention, and you've chosen to pick up something I made, and for that, I am honored and grateful.

Because I am indebted to you, I want to be extremely respectful of your time. This book is for leaders. If you don't think you are a leader, or have no plans of becoming one, you can send this book back. I'll personally refund it. The leaders who will find this book most useful are entrepreneurs who own and manage their own businesses, but C-level executives, nonprofit founders, pastors, teachers, and anyone who wears a uniform will relate to some of the stories and can benefit from the lessons contained in these pages.

When I lived in Las Vegas I became very involved in the nonprofit American Dream U, which helps many thousands of military veterans and their families build their dream lives and their own businesses. Everyone from Joe Rogan to Grant Cardone to Tim Ferris has been involved in American Dream U: helping American heroes create something special of their own. It was an honor to be a part of that, not so much because of our headlining speakers, but because I got to serve my tribe: self-starters with a heart to serve others. If you consider yourself a servant leader or aspire to become one, welcome to my tribe. Let's build something together!

Chapter 1

Put God First

"Faith is taking the first step even when you don't see the whole staircase."

Martin Luther King, Jr.

Tim's Tutors began on accident. That's not something most entrepreneurs will admit. If I want to gain your trust, shouldn't I say that I had this dream to be a business owner and educator since I was five? That wasn't the case though. I saw a need, a need with a very human face, and I found a solution.

Lee was one of the first people I met when I moved to Las Vegas. He and his father had a small carpet cleaning business, and I hit it off with both of them right away. Las

LEAD, SERVE, WIN.

Vegas schools had a 50% dropout rate at the time, and were teaching values that went against everything Lee's family believed in, so they decided to homeschool his younger brother. The problem is, they knew nothing about math, and books and videos weren't helping.

My claim to fame in education circles is that I went from Special Ed to Ivy League – literally. I was held back after kindergarten, placed in something called "pre-first" grade, and spent most of elementary school being told that I had a learning disability. How I completed three college degrees and a postgraduate program at Cornell University could be the subject of another book – and probably will be - but suffice it to say that I knew about math, and I knew about falling behind in it. I wasn't looking to make money from it, but they told me they insisted.

A couple weeks later, I was at a yoga studio learning how to stand on my head. My teacher, Marissa, invited me out to eat after class, but I told her I was already booked with math tutoring. I'll never forget her reply.

"Can you help my kids too? I don't have a lot of money, but I can pay in vegetables."

Quick backstory, we were in Las Vegas, and Marissa had her own little organic farm where she would grow vegetables. This garden was just incredible. It had a massive variety of spinach, eggplants, and whatnot. Naturally, I couldn't say no and I quite literally got paid in vegetables.

Even around this time, I was not even trying to make a living out of this. From there, I started gaining a bit of a reputation. Add to that the fact that these families wanted me to be more regular and teach their kids, and it was becoming more evident; I was good at this teaching stuff.

I started putting some ads at Craigslist. Mind you, I had already gained some knowledge and experience with marketing, and back then, not everyone knew about Google Ads or Facebook Ads.

Soon, I landed myself with a third client. As fate would have it, this client was a little chaotic and I had to fire them as a client. It's not easy saying no to regular money, expecially when it's from someone who had been with you from the start. The fact was that they wanted me to do things I didn't sign up for - like designing their website for them fixing their printer, and so much more. Letting this family know that I no longer had time for them was a difficult lesson in setting boundaries. Later, when I read the book "Boundaries" by Henry Cloud and John Townsend, I learned that most people are terrified of saying "no."

Of course, I was respectful when I ended that relationship. After all, I had served them for years, and I was grateful that they took a chance on me when I was just starting. Most importantly, over the years that I was with them, they referred me to a ton of clients who ended up being much better fits. My struggles made a lot more sense when I trusted God for the outcome. Embrace your downturns!

My fourth client was a true Godsend. When I met Kim and her family, I was just starting to establish myself in Las Vegas. Kim was a senior VP at Wynn Resorts, and her husband Harry was CFO of Caesars entertainment. More important than Kim's connections though, was her character. Kim offered to pay me double what I had been asking because she wanted her family to come first. What an example for anyone trying to run a business or a family! It's become cliché to compare work with family, but she really did treat me like part of the family. My own family was on the east coast, so I spent many a holiday at Kim's. The education I got at Superbowl parties and Easter breakfasts at Kim's house was worth more than what I learned at Cornell graduate school. One Thanksgiving dinner that stands out, when I had just started building my team of tutors, Harry pulled me aside to teach me the top lesson he got from his Harvard MBA: hire fast, fire faster.

In addition to telling me how to build a team, Kim and her family showed me how. Her onboarding process was short, but intense. I know now that she had plenty of more qualified people available to tutor her kids, but nobody was as hungry as I was. In fact, as they got older over the years, some of their subjects were outside of my area of expertise, and I was able to bring in members of my team to help take over, but she always preferred to deal with me personally, because she knew I would do whatever it took to get her family the results they needed. In fact, Kim made a habit of texting and emailing me every week, and eventually I got the hint and started to be the one who reached out first. Even the best help will get distracted, so make sure to check in with them regularly to reignite their passion for your mission.

Finding God

Here's a fun fact: I was raised in a church-going family. My mother was actually a Sunday School teacher, but eventually stopped going when she got a new job and started working nights. She would still send us with the neighbor who taught the kids' choir.

I church hopped for a while, sometimes going years in between services. I met a lot of great people from all denominations. I got baptized in a small church in Asbury Park on the Jersey shore, and I moved to Las Vegas shortly thereafter. Moving to Vegas after reconnecting with God after a long hiatus is not something I'd recommend for everyone, but thankfully I found Central Church when I arrived.

I immediately got involved, and when Pastor Shawn told me he wanted to start a college for the church, I was on board 100%. I later went on to use my experience helping start Central College and Central Academy to help build schools and orphanages around the globe.

When you stop worrying about yourself and start helping others, your plate becomes full automatically!

Connect to God – Find Your True Self

What people fail to realize is that the more connected they are to God, the more connected they become to their inner selves. When you start putting God first, you start helping many around you. As a result, God helps you in His own ways. This is why those who donate, give charity, and help others are always the ones who go on to become huge success stories we learn about in our history books.

Then, there is the fact that when your faith in God is strong, other people sense that. This is why I was able to find myself comfortable around these people because my faith in God was growing stronger and stronger.

God has never let anyone on their own. He would always show signs of His presence and His never-ending support and love to those who seek His help. This is why it is said:

Ask; and it will be given to you. Seek; and you shall find!

TIM PRUNYI

There was a time where I was completely burned out from working seven days a week, 10 hours a day, driving across town every rush-hour, and managing half-a-dozen more tutors doing the same thing. I felt like I would lose my bearings and end up in losses. It was through me asking God for His help that I was able to learn about delegating my time-consuming activities. Because of that, I was then able to travel for one whole year.

Now, before you assume that I was just enjoying my time, let me clarify. While I was travelling, I was helping others set up schools. I set up schools in Thailand, the first place I visited, and then The Philippines, Nicaragua, and Mexico. While the business was sustaining itself, there wasn't much that was coming in for me as I was investing all of that helping others set up schools. For a while, I was just living every day on land. I was a backpacking traveler.

During my time in these places, people from the States would reach out to me, requesting me to come back and help them with their projects. Eventually, I decided I was happy with what I did, but it was now time to head back and go home.

My year-long journey wasn't my idea – It was that of God. He wanted me to go out there and help many others. He wanted me to go out there and plant seeds so that others could then take benefit from them. Not many people tend to get this chance, and I was fortunate enough that I did.

LEAD, SERVE, WIN.

This entire year also allowed me to finally break the dichotomy of wanting something for myself or not. Travelling these lands with nothing but a backpack and campaign most of the time allowed me to realize how much I would appreciate having a home. There is always a middle ground between "Me, me, me" and "give, give, give" and that's what I discovered.

While you should continue to give as much as you can, keep something for yourself as well. God doesn't want His creation to live in dirt. We are meant to live in abundance, not scarcity.

You Need Faith – You Need God

Given the recent time that we all had to go through, a lot of people lost hope of ever seeing a better tomorrow. A lot of people would just run around, screaming, and panicking as it was the end of the world. It wasn't – It isn't. All you need is faith; All you need is God. If you started a business, there's a good chance that God put that idea into your head. Have faith that He will give you what you need to win as long as you follow through.

When you have faith, you know you can expect a better tomorrow. Why? Because you believe in God and in your faith. The stronger your faith, the more you manifest the goodness in life. That's the power of faith and how it allows your mind to manifest all your dreams, goals, and ambitions into a living, breathing reality.

Life is full of uncertainty. We have absolutely no idea how the next hour would turn out to be, let alone the next year or decade. When you have faith, you know it will come, you know it will be good, and you know what you are hoping to find there. If things don't go the way you plan, you have your faith to lean on to and God to ask for help. Does He help? Always. While His help may not be evident right away, it makes perfect sense as time goes on.

It could be anything. If you didn't get it, it's probably for the best, and it is only because you chose to put your faith in God. When you do that, He isn't going to leave you be and let you suffer through misery.

One of my favorite podcasts is the Momentum Podcast by Alex Charfen. I had read his book The Entrepreneurial Personality Type and been listening to Alex's podcast for years, when I saw a job posting on his Instagram. At the time, I was in the Philippines building schools and orphanages, but I had been such a fan of Alex's for so long that I felt that I had to reach out and give it a shot. The internet was inconsistent at best, and Alex has a famously intense onboarding process: he really wants to see how you work. Despite everything stacked against me, I got the job, and got to be part of the creative team for one of my favorite creators. I came back to the US and started my dream job working on The Billionaire

LEAD, SERVE, WIN.

Code. I thought it was God's will. Alex was an inspirational leader, but my heart was still with the orphans. We parted was friends and I went on to help build more schools and orphanages, this time in Mexico. I thought that God wanted material success for me the moment it presented itself through Alex, but He was really in that still small voice telling me to help the children.

The Takeaway

Not everyone will be called to work with orphans, but we all have a special gift and calling. Material success did come to me, but not the way I had thought it would. I had to take that break from building schools to understand how much I needed those orphans in that phase of my life.

I'm grateful I went back into the field, because within a few short years it became very difficult to travel. Much of the world was being locked down at the start of 2020, and businesses were being shut down and going under. Tim's Tutors – the venture that funded my missions work and allowed me to travel – was in serious danger. My friend Clay, whose friend Shaan gotten an investment from Mark Cuban on Shark Tank, asked me if I could come on board and build them a team of the world's top educators. I was able to bring my people: both clients and staff. This allowed me to bring security to the people whom I was responsible for.

- Have no God's before God
- Seek first the Kingdom of Heaven
- Everything will be provided for

Write: What have you made more important than God in your own life?

Chapter 2

Progress, Not Perfection

We human beings are far too eager to search for perfection that we tend to lose progress in the process. For this very reason, a vast majority of people have never started with their ideas, dreams, and goals because they were far too busy waiting for "the perfect time." That never comes, and if it does, it is always too late.

This chapter, therefore, is a perfect way to understand why should you prioritize progress and not perfection. There is reason, there is logic, and above all, there are results if you do it the right way.

Perfection is an Elusive Dream

It is true. The idea of perfection is one that evades everyone. No matter what you try, there is always something that doesn't fit the picture. There is always something that makes you think, "Ah! I could do better." That's a sign that you are trying too hard to chase the idea that is, by its very nature, never going to materialize.

The Wright Brothers designed the world's first aircraft. Was it perfect in any shape of form? No. What matters is that they did it anyway. Over the course of a century, the design was then improved and continues to do so even today. Similarly, the very first computer that was created. It literally needed an entire room just so it could be housed. Was that a perfect design? No, but someone still did it anyway. I can name a million other inventions that could have never happened had their respective inventors chased perfection. Instead, they focused on progress.

The business that hired me as a Prep expert, their entire foundation was based on the idea that the founder ended up with a perfect score on their SAT. While he has a pretty impressive story, it does become shallow with time when you go on to replicate and mass produce that.

My task was simply to mass produce the very same results. This meant that I had to hire one person per day for the better part of a year. That's a lot of people.

LEAD, SERVE, WIN.

Most of the people we hired ended up being hired based on their test scores. With time, I put in a very good system in place that would help smoothen the process. From job posting to screening the right candidates, it was all there.

The problem was that test scores doesn't always answer the question. I can score really good, but that doesn't mean I have the ability to explain things or teach things to others better.

Things that come naturally to me are the hardest things to explain to someone else!

My tutoring went really well because I had struggled a lot back in the days. Being a child that was enrolled in a special ed and then making my way into Ivy League, that never comes without going through the struggles that I did. During the interviews, I would try to flip the script and avoid looking at the test scores. I would present them with a random problem and ask them to explain the same to me as if I was a student.

Do you see what I was doing here? I was ignoring perfection in favor of progress. One candidate may have the perfect SAT scores, but if someone with a lower SAT score can explain things better, I want the person who can communicate the solution ten times out of ten.

TIM PRUNYI

Test scores, like any credentials age poorly. How many engineers remember all the math they had to study to get their degree? Rather than let credentials speak for themselves, I made sure that our interview process included a simulation of the actual job. This is what I call the "technical interview." With standardized tests like the SAT and ACT, this meant that I had to give them some of the hardest questions from the real tests – tests notorious for trick questions and misdirection. To be clear, this was not an attempt to "trick" the candidates. That would serve neither them nor our organization. It was a simulation of a very real part of the job. To make my people feel more comfortable, I would even comment that many people on our team, or even myself had been caught off guard by some of the trickier questions, and that I wasn't looking for perfection from them. This put them at ease, and made them feel more connected to me and my team. I even let them know that they would have access to answer keys and step-by-step solutions to all problems if they needed them, and that I was always open to input, and might pick their brain on improving the step-by-step solutions. This made them feel like they could make a difference in what at first seemed like a monolithic organization. Letting candidates know that their voice would be heard, and their suggestions could be implemented helped them get excited for the job.

LEAD, SERVE, WIN.

If they would get the question wrong, it wouldn't bother me at all. My aim was to test their resiliency, to see how quick they would recover from the situation.

People make mistakes all the time, but the art lies in how they recover from those mistakes. Little things like, "This is why we show all the steps, so that we don't lose track of things," go on to really catch my attention.

When you need to build a team, you need to follow a golden rule:

Hire fast; fire faster!

This may seem a little harsh, but here's the thing. If you have a person that is not a good fit for your team, the longer they stay, the more damage it can cause. Similarly, you can't really leave a position open for long because the workload may eventually become too much for the current members of the team to handle. Therefore, you need to ensure you hire people fast too.

In general, people tend to wait a very long time to wait for that "Perfect" person that would be a "Perfect" fit for the team. This wait game can stretch out to be fairly long. I know because we were waiting for the miniature version of the founder to show up out of the blue so that we could hire them. We were waiting for this perfect avatar to present themselves before us and say "I am willing to do all that the founder had done for $20 bucks an hour."

No one in their right mind would do that. In fact, if there are miniature versions of the founder, they are busy running their own companies, not being employed at $20 bucks an hour. Gary Vaynerchuck says that nobody will ever care about your business as much as you do, and this matches pretty well with my own experience.

With me, I had a lot of luck with students and people who had recently gone through the test as they were more up-to-speed with the process. Those who had gone through their tests ages ago were very rusty. I don't blame them, that's just how things work.

When you are in college or just started your professional career, $20 bucks an hour isn't really bad at all. This is why the younger people that I hired went on to become superstars just because they were hungry to learn, adapt, and take up on challenges.

I remember how I once hired a brilliant woman who graduated from Yale. I fought to give her raises every step of the way. However, I knew that she would eventually go on to bigger and better things. That's the key when hiring the best of the best: opportunities follow top performers, so you need to pay them really well and making working with you really fun.

LEAD, SERVE, WIN.

Of course, not everyone is going to be a top performer, regardless of Ivy League education or experience with big name corporations. Every company and role will have unique red flags to look for in candidates, but some are universal: lack of drive, lack of commitment, lack of enthusiasm. If somebody shows up late to your interview, what do you think they're going to do with your clients?

You cannot teach someone how to be punctual – You either are, or you aren't!

I am willing to teach you mathematics but I cannot teach you human skills like how to talk to someone, how to respond to situations, or how to be punctual. These are core values that you need to work on your own. My job is limited to training you how to be an effective tutor, not how to lead life. That part is yours to handle and yours to work on.

When someone is paying you something, you are meant to bring your best. However, if you aren't there yet, there is always someone to guide you accordingly. I do the same with those who are good enough but need some training. I would be more than happy to mentor them and teach them to make it all the way through. Of course, during that phase, they won't be on the payroll until they are fully ready.

You Need Driven People

The idea is to find people that feel like your mission is already on their heart. There are people who have their calling in teaching others. It just comes naturally to them. In fact, there are those who would be willing to do it for free (not that I am suggesting you don't pay them).

Find people that would do it for free, then pay them well!

This is exactly what I found in my intern Isabella – an enthusiastic MBA candidate. Isabella taught hundreds of students as a volunteer. She was exactly the right person to train to lead a team of hundreds of tutors, and she was fully deserving of a comfortable life while she did God's work. I advocated for her to advance quickly in her new corporate career.

You will never be good at something unless you love doing that particular job. You need to find people who are driven and are willing to bring everything they have and deliver.

There was a brilliant Harvard student on my team named David. From day one, I knew this guy had it in him. Over the years, he has proven himself to be a worthy addition to the team. I decided to recommend giving him a raise.

"Did he ask for a raise?"

"No! I believe he should get one though. He has earned it."

Here's the thing, if you are waiting for someone to ask for a raise, you are already too late!

If you notice something, reward them. There must always be a reward for those who are putting in their efforts to make things work.

You Don't Know What You Don't Know

When it comes to writing resumes, I know a lot of people would just try and check every box the exists, just to improve their chances. While I am not saying this is the case with everyone, a lot of people would try and put in things that aren't even true. Why? Because they are hoping to show themselves as the perfect candidate for the job.

When building ed-tech companies, I had a lot of pressure to hire based on vanity metrics like top SAT scores and graduate degrees. Those things are great, and I hired a lot of people who could check those boxes, but there were far more important things to look for:

1. How they present themselves on a call.
2. How did they respond to being stumped?

3. Could they explain deep concepts simply?
4. How would they correct their own mistakes?
5. Would they show up on time? Early?
6. How quickly could they figure out our software?

    I would much rather have someone who is coachable with reasonable test scores from a decent school than someone with perfect test scores from a top college that makes excuses for being late and shows up unprepared.

    A strong team must maintain a balance. This means that you cannot expect to hire someone who is just another version of you. If you are someone who is constantly seeking to hire people just like you, it won't work. What you truly need is coachable people that are your opposite in certain respects. After all, you're not hiring people to take over the things you love. As long as they are coachable, eager, and willing to learn, they will go on to provide that delicate balance to the team.

    Stop duplicating yourself unless you actually need a successor. At the risk of declaring everyone special snowflakes, each individual does have unique talents, quirks, and skills. This isn't about hiring for diversity's sake. It's about building a team that will complement your strengths and compensate for your weaknesses.

LEAD, SERVE, WIN.

Know Where to Focus

Sometimes well meaning people can become poison to a business. This is especially true with social justice warriors and other types of crusaders. Don't let these people near your company's mission and vision statements. They will have you chasing so many priorities that your team will forget why your even exists. God bless them, but I have seen how they have ended up derailing companies. All they did was to make everything as their primary focus except for the reason the company exists.

Don't get me wrong; it doesn't matter what priorities someone has. I have my own set of rules and beliefs and someone else may have their own. However, in order for us to work together, there must be a common ground we both can agree upon and work at. If that common ground isn't there, it won't work at all.

Things are really infested in the education system. I consider myself to be the odd ball. While everyone talks about which vaccine they ended up getting, I am more focused on talking about the students.

Our mission is to solve the problems of those we serve. We are here to focus on one thing, not fix all the problems of the world. Focusing on what you need is essential because otherwise, you would be trying to do everything. When that happens, you will miss every mark.

In my undergraduate years, I joined an environmental group called Take Back the Tap. This organization was all about being sustainable and not creating waste by using plastic water bottles. It's a very practical way of helping the environment with very tangible results. The problem with environmental groups is that they are terrible at focusing on their actual mission. Meetings devolved into discussions of "allyship" with other organizations and causes that had absolutely zero to do with eliminating waste from disposable water bottles. While we did a lot of good getting some water refilling stations installed on campus, the group fell apart because it couldn't keep the main thing the main thing.

You need to have a single mission to accomplish. How you accomplish it is up to you. The moment you make the water muddy, you end up losing core people!

The Takeaway

Progress means you just get started with the first possible step, regardless of how far that seems from the end. Then you take the next step, then the next. Before you know it, you've achieved some massive goals. If you wait for perfection, you are probably never going to move forward. This isn't an excuse to do a bad job. This is a cure to procrastination.

LEAD, SERVE, WIN.

In Ancient Greece there were cults that all but worshipped math; they were obsessed with the perfection of numbers. Some of them became so extreme that they renounced the physical world – reality itself. Many of us have a similar obsession today. We pass on excellent candidates, holding out for the perfect fit. We delay important projects, hoping for the perfect moment. While caution is often wise, procrastination usually goes well beyond caution.

I have seen this everywhere. Many people who set out to acquire perfect results, they come back with no results at all. Even if they are able to find people that are just like them, they end up disagreeing on almost everything. It becomes a war of egos as opposed to an organization using its resources to play its due part and provide services. Therefore, it is very important to understand:

1. Progress, not perfection
2. Find one thing to focus on at a time
3. Stop waiting for the perfect moment and take action!

Write: What am I putting off because it isn't the "perfect moment."

Chapter 3

You Will Be Hated

When you have strong beliefs and a strong culture, you go on to create some hatred and friction. Let me be honest, being hated isn't fun. It sucks to be hated, but when you follow your goals, visions, and develop a strong culture, it is only natural to expect some hatred.

Society teaches that it is nice to be liked by everyone, but the very same society has never once found a person they can all agree to love and like. There is always someone out there who will hate you for who you are. This could be out of jealousy, out of some personal difference, or it could just be downright pointless.

Find Your Tribe

We are community-based creatures. You can try and do whatever you can, but there is absolutely nothing you can do to satisfy everyone. You can invent something so revolutionary that it gives free electricity to the world, and you will find people who will say how you are creating a monopoly or how you are damaging the environment, even if you aren't. That's the kind of society we live in. Therefore, why bother? Instead of trying to please everyone and wasting your energy, resources, and time, find your tribe first. When you are surrounded with people that are like-minded, you are bound to be more productive and experience more growth in all quarters of life.

Every city, every town within our country is big enough to have a tribe or two that resonates with each one of us. All we need to do is to go online and find them.

I live in the suburbs of Tampa, Florida. After many years of living in the heart of Las Vegas, I wanted to live in a small, quiet neighborhood by the water. Even in my beachside getaway, there are dozens of tribes all around me: conservatives, liberals, patriots, communists, religious denominations of every shape and size. I love to go to live entrepreneurship workshops, retreats, and events. I consider these pep rallies to get filled up with the energy I need to go back home and execute my vision. I see a lot of people attend these events and not go home and execute though. If that's you, you aren't alone.

When you are vocal about your core values, what they can do and what they can't, you end up creating some hatred. This also happens to those who become more and more successful. The more success you garner, the more hatred you find around you. While nobody wants to be hated, the fact is that this hatred is only natural.

People tend to see what you have in that moment, but they are not willing to see what you had to go through in order to get there. That's the part they conveniently choose not to take into consideration.

When you find your tribe, you automatically start mingling with people that are better able to understand you and help you. These are people that have already been through similar experiences and know exactly how much effort goes into reaching to a place where you may currently be at. They won't hate you – Not a bit – but instead, they will help you go to the next level.

I generally tend to avoid groups or tribes where I know I will most likely be hated. Why waste time trying to mingle in a crowd that isn't even ready to listen to me or work with me?

Know Yourself – Be Yourself

Once, I was in Mexico and working with the orphans there. For some reason, I had decided to take a beach day. It had been months since I took one and I felt like I really need a beach day for a change. As I packed, I decided to take my laptop with me. At the beach, I decided to post something on Facebook. This was a post that was posted by some lady regarding the sexual revolution and how it had done more harm than good. She mentioned how this sexual revolution wasn't working out. My idea was to share this post by the lady so that her voice could further be shared with the audience. I had no idea of the kind of hatred I would end up getting from people on my Facebook.

People started being so vocal against my post. They would say things that showed genuine hatred. One of these people was a good friend of mine who had donated an amount for the orphans I was working with. It read, "Now I regret sending money to your orphanage."

Those orphans never wrote that post and nor did I. All I did was to share something that touched me and made me feel like I should share further with the audience. My goal was never to upset anyone, but it was evident that I had struck quite a few nerves. This was a young woman in South America expressing her feelings, not mine.

When you stand for something, something within you wakes up, and when that happens, expect a lot of hatred coming your way. However, instead of focusing on that hatred, look at the positives. There are those who would see eye-to-eye with your views and appreciate you. They are usually your tribe members. They are the kind of people that would help you be a better version of you and not try to suppress your thoughts, your feelings or your dreams.

Think about it; an average person sitting on a dinner table with his family suddenly decides to make an announcement.

"Okay. I am going to quit my job and become an entrepreneur."

This is his wish, his vision, and his dream. I would say "Go for it!" I might even help him understand how things work. However, that won't be the first reaction he would get.

"Are you insane?"
"Have you lost it?"
"Why? Why would you do that?"
"Oh, you don't want to do that. Trust me."

Most of these people immediately showing resentment is a clear sign that they aren't willing to see eye-to-eye. I am not saying that they will never understand your vision, but that's just how society is.

You can either fear being hated and hate your life later on, or you can let the hatred pour in, do what you want to do, and love your life later on! It's your choice!

When you are transparent from the very beginning and crystal clear about what you aim for, what you are okay with and what you aren't okay with, you are going to set precedence. Yes, you will immediately attract more hatred right away, but at least, you were being honest from the start.

I remember once when someone from work "advised" me to change my profile picture on my LinkedIn account. This was a picture of me making a goofy face while holding a pen and a calculator. I wasn't smoking weed, pot, or doing anything that was vulgar or obscene in any way. It was just me, expressing a side of me that I know I have. They quite literally said:

"It's not professional."

I'm sorry, but I wasn't working at LinkedIn and nor was I going to change my picture because someone thought I was not being professional. If I was smoking weed or doing drugs in my picture, it would have made perfect sense to update that. In my case, it felt a bit awkward and somewhat upsetting to hear that people would go to such lengths to show their resentment towards me. My LinkedIn profile had nothing to do with them or the company.

"If the world hates you, remember that it hated me first."

John 15:18-27

Hatred follows success. The more success you get, the more hatred you find. It's just a natural thing and you can't really avoid that. The best thing you can do is to know who you truly are and stick with it.

Back when I was starting Tim's Tutors, I would post quite a lot of stuff on how the schooling system in Nevada sucked. The numbers showed that it had the worst drop-out rate, which stood at a whopping 50%.

The school system was doing everything except for what it was actually supposed to do – To educate the children. All it would do was to find ways to make itself look good in the eyes of the government and the public. However, numbers don't lie, and I knew exactly where those numbers were.

As someone who was offering a solution to that problem, I was quite clear and vocal about it. What's funny is that I went on to have contracts with the school district, which was somewhat fun.

These contracts were lucrative, and I honestly thought I would be able to do a good job and help the school system restore its reputation. However, I learned that was not going to happen at all. The contracts were absolutely not worth my time and my skills.

When you offer your services but you are made to follow someone else's directives, you immediately find yourself in a tight spot. You can't even do what you know is the right thing to do. Everyone is literally at the mercy of certain political players that can decide, if they even do that, whether the school should do this or that. I am sorry, but I cannot see myself working in such a system at all. If I put in my efforts, I must be able to produce results based on my input, not based on somebody else's wishes. Naturally, I walked away.

Your Core Values Matter

Part of knowing yourself is to know your core values. Once again, if you know your core values, you are going to find resentment creeping its way into your life once again. Why? Because you would know what is acceptable to you and what isn't, and that may not sit well with everyone around you.

People would love for us to do everything they ask for. They would ask us to help them do their assignments, write their reports, help them get hired in your firm, or even partner up on deals where they have literally nothing of value to offer. If you know your core values, you are most likely going to say "No" to them straight away, in a respectful manner – of course! However, let me ask you this; would they take it nicely?

In most cases, no. They would storm out of the office, start gossiping about you on the office floor, or even block you off from their contact lists. The problems increase ten folds if you are the owner of the firm. You become that "typical boss that everybody hates" and you won't be able to do much about it. Here's my advice; don't do anything about it. Stick with your core values because your entire business is essentially in alignment with those values. If you blur the edges once, you will open a floodgate of problems.

Breaking the Ranks

Some of the most inspiring men and women that I've met have been through that non-profit American Dream U. This organization helps veterans start their own businesses. I would urge anyone who hasn't heard of American Dream U to look them up along with founder, Phil Randazzo. Phil has written a plethora of books and put together events where entrepreneurs like Grant Cardone and Ryan Holiday shared stages with top military brass and C-level executives from huge corporations like Starbucks. The combination of live

LEAD, SERVE, WIN.

events and online courses launched many heroes into a dream career, where they could not only find, but build their tribe. The live events were like pep-rallies, where people could get inspired, network, and pump each other up to achieve greatness. The courses provided actionable next steps to follow to build your dream team.

Structure is useful for anyone trying to get things done, but for anyone coming out of the military, it is life itself. Veterans have chains of command and standard operating procedures stamped onto their souls, so it can be very scary starting your own thing. The beauty of American Dream U is that veterans get to create their own structure and create their own tribe. Much as veterans crave structure, they also crave freedom - this is especially true for veterans with the drive to start their own businesses. To be honest, we all need structure and discipline, but the best structure and discipline come from within.

I met a lot of veterans who were at the top but had no idea what to do next. While they had all the freedom in the world, they had no vision. They would ask me for help to try and uncover their vision, but to be honest, I cannot dictate anyone what their vision may be. It is up to each one of us to figure that part out.

The live events were designed to get people excited and fill their spirits. Even Joe Rogan got a chance to share some inspirational words with our veterans to put them in the right mindset before the real work began. Through the words and encouragement offered by these powerhouses, these ex-military personnel were then able to find their own calling. This is something that had to be done because people who have served in military are programmed to follow that chain of command and receive orders. When they step out of the military, they must take over the top spot, issue commands, set missions, and do all of that. This is something that they aren't trained to do in the military; this is what American Dream U was designed to do. It helped these veterans to find out what they must target and help them achieve those goals.

I was born to be an educator, but I hate what the education industry has become. Some of us are naturally inclined to be educators, but don't fit in with the entrenched ideologies that currently dominate the education system from top to bottom. Despite my disdain for the current system, I was born with the ability to find the best in people and bring it out of them.

I was not the perfect student. Before I found myself in the Ivy Leagues, I paid my dues in special education: as a student. I know that kids, half of the time, don't even want to listen any way, meaning that more than 50% of the efforts are generally wasted. This mixture of being a teacher and an entrepreneur is just what I needed to make things work for me and the students.

LEAD, SERVE, WIN.

I am a teacher and as a teacher, it is hard to teach someone how to be a teacher. You either know it or you don't. This is why I would hire people that had this ability of teaching and explaining things to the students as opposed to those who had perfect SAT scores. I wasn't filling the roles; I was focused on hiring the right people for the right job. It's to feed into that vision, to help solve a problem.

How to Set Your Vision?

Setting a vision may be easier for people who do not have military experiences. However, it is still tricky for most people. Most people have zero idea of what they are aiming for. If you think you want to do something in life to make more money, that's not a vision. However, if you are aiming to solve a problem you have identified by employing the right people and working towards that solution which, in turn, will go on to help many others; that's a vision.

People need to define their objectives in clear terms. They must be able to recall their objective from the back of their heads like they would recall their names when asked for them.

For the first 20 to 25 years, others have been defining your objectives for you.

"You must go to college."

"You must get a degree."
"You need to accomplish this mission."

For the first leg of the journey, you have been taking orders. However, now, it's your turn to define your own objectives. You can, and you will!

Start small because it is better to work with. Instead of jumping straight on a larger-than-life goal, start small. You don't have to worry about anything else as long as this small objective of yours is being accomplished.

Take a leaf from the book of mountaineering. These professionals may eventually aim to summit peaks like K2 or Mount Everest, but they don't go big immediately. They start small.

"Let's take that hill first."

They would focus their attention, their energy, and utilize their resources to hike a hill. Once done, they can then set their target to something a little bigger. From one to another, hills after hills, they will eventually be able to target the bigger ones. Even when they are out there to summit these monstrous peaks, they start small and plan systematically.

LEAD, SERVE, WIN.

"Okay. Today, we will hike to base camp 2."

Once that is done, they can then move on to base camp 3, 4, and eventually summit the peaks.

When you start small, you go on to gain motivation to do something a bit bigger. Without motivation, you cannot expect yourself to achieve much in life, and there is no better way to gain motivation than to accumulate smaller victories.

To help you move forward, it may be a good idea to have some assistance, someone to guide you whether it really is your mission. This is particularly true for veterans as this helps you establish some roles within the organization. Having an advisor or an assistant can help you work out what your vision truly is and what isn't. Based on your core values, you can work out your missions, set your objectives and goals, and then go on to achieve those, one by one. Remember, we are not aiming for perfection here; we want progress.

You may set end up setting a mission and it happens to be something that you don't really believe in. Regardless, you do it anyways because it sounds nice. That's okay because that's still some progress. You are moving in some direction, and some is better than none at all.

I cannot emphasize enough on how much trial and error is undervalued. It is through this process of trial and error that you refine your visions, your missions, and your objectives. It is through this trial and error that you get to learn so much more about what you want to accomplish, what you can accomplish, and what you should avoid.

Do Not Be Intimidated

It is fairly easy for people to be intimidated by the amount of hatred they end up getting when they start doing something that they believe is right. However, this part comes naturally, and I wish there was a better way. Since there isn't, we entrepreneurs stick with our objectives, our principles, core values and goals.

Take a look at Elon Musk. He is technically the most hated person on social media these days. However, at the very same time, he also happens to be the most talked about and liked person on social media too. A single tweet from him ends up getting insanely high number of interactions.

Despite all that hate, despite the massive failures he encountered, did he ever quit? No. If anything, he continues to persevere and dream bigger, aim for bigger results, and has already stunned the world through Tesla and the Space X program.

I may like him or I may not like him, but I acknowledge the fact that this guy is successful. If anyone was to ask me to name the most successful person today, I might probably name him.

LEAD, SERVE, WIN.

Then, there is the fact that his life, his story, and his lessons that he often talks about offers a lot of things for everyone to learn from. Sure enough, I have learned a few things myself. However, just because I am picking up on some of the lessons and learning it for my own good does not mean I would go on to endorse every single thing he says or does.

What's really strange is how people would waste their energies trying to talk bad about him. It is saddening to see that they hold so much hatred for someone that is successful, and the most hurtful part is that they aren't ready to talk sense either.

To begin with, he is not that important to me. He is just another entrepreneur that is massively successful. That is it. However, people go on to argue with me, trying their hardest to convince me and make me hate him. Why? I am not idolizing him, and whatever he does, I am not bothered by that. Why waste your energy spreading hatred on rumors and gossips you might have picked up from questionable sources?

Being hated comes with being successful!

In most cases, those who hate Elon are probably the people that have never done anything like him. They loathe the fact that he went on to enjoy success of unimaginable magnitude whereas they are still working through their 9 to 5 jobs or running smaller businesses. This isn't a comparison game guys! If you really want to compare something with Elon or any other successful entrepreneur, compare your actions, your thought process and your approach to work with theirs. That's a productive thing to do because that's where you will actually pick up those little clues to success. Remember, every success story leaves behind some golden nuggets for you to consume and grow. Instead of focusing all your attention on hatred, use the energy to find out ways how you can do something like them but in a better way.

      Another exceptional man who has drawn a lot of hate lately is Chris Pratt. The actor who made his name on the cult NBC show Parks and Recreation and became a household name with The Lego Movie, Guardians of the Galaxy, and Jurassic World was beloved by Hollywood as the quintessential guy next door. When Chris started speaking openly about his Christian faith, organized campaigns against him sprung up online. My goal here isn't to get you to feel bad for a tech billionaire and a movie star. Quite the opposite. These men are proof that being hated is a sign of success. Embrace the fact that you will be hated the more significant you become to the world around you.

      When I was able to build my team and bring it to where it is now, I ended up creating a rift between me and the former director of operations. It was he who was initially tasked to put together a team before they decided to bring me in and do the same thing. This person was extremely critical of every single thing that I was doing. The fact was that I had succeeded where he failed. He was not able to put together a team because he would take a very long time just to schedule interviews whereas I was always moving at a faster pace.

Then, there was the process that was involved. It was a very complicated and confusing process, which is probably why most of the candidates would never show up. When I came in, I redesigned the process. I brought in interns, contractors, and employees, and I was able to build a real team.

"Well, where are you storing the test scores?"

Just like this question, he would come up with something to criticize me over at random. It was evident that whatever I would do, it wouldn't please him at all. The fact is that he could have actually done all of this himself but couldn't do so.

He had a 2-year project to hire someone as an intern for a specific role. He never had any success. One day, we had a meeting where I asked if he would like me to take over this part and find an intern. I only wanted to help him overcome a problem he was facing, but he still decided to redirect me to something that was unproductive in nature.

"No! That's not going to help you."

As it turns out, he was trying to work with his process whereas the only problem there was the process itself.

"Do you want me to get this done? Yes, or no?"

Eventually, the founder intervened and gave me a green light after which I was able to get the job done far more effectively and in a far more efficient manner. All it took me was two weeks to find an intern. However, during this intern's onboarding process, the guy decided to quit. As a result, she ended up becoming my intern.

The Takeaway

When you become mission-driven, expect to make some enemies within the organization. There are those who may not see eye-to-eye with your vision, your mission, or your goal. They would try and question you, try to derail you, but that's just a sign for you to know that you are doing something right.

LEAD, SERVE, WIN.

I have learned through a lot of experience that hatred is real and it develops fairly quick. Therefore, the pointers I want you to take away from this chapter are:

1. Do not be intimidated
2. People who hate your mission will hate you automatically
3. You can win some people over, but not everyone.
4. If you succeed where others fail, they will hate you
5. Learn how to set your vision and work on your mission regardless of the hatred that may come towards you

Write: What have I avoided doing because of how I thought other people would react?

Chapter 4

Your Body is a Temple

Back in the days when the world was ruled by rulers and emperors, we had kings and queens ruling over us. These people were strong leaders. You couldn't be a king just because you inherited yourself the throne; you needed grit and strength. If you were someone people believed in and trusted to protect them and provide them with their necessities, they would follow you.

On the other hand, if you are weak and you don't really do much to change your habits, two things are going to happen:

1. People will hate you and probably overthrow your regime

LEAD, SERVE, WIN.

2. You are most likely going to die a lot sooner than you might expect

Your body is a temple and it is so because if you feed your body with all the right things, you gain the ability to do things that will help you lead and conquer challenges. You can't expect to be obese and be able to manage a business with 100% of your energy, and nor can you do that if you are underweight.

What you need is to take care of your body because everything else depends on it.

Your Success Hinges on Your Health

They say that health is the purest form of wealth, and they aren't kidding about that. If you are healthy enough, you can virtually anything that you set your mind to. However, if you are someone who isn't healthy enough, you would be:

- Drowsy
- Lethargic
- Out of energy
- Lacking focus
- Tired
- Stressed

- Ill
- Anxious
- Ill-tempered

That is just scratching the surface. You would run into a world full of problems that would quite literally restrict your movements and your thought process.

I know this because when I was a kid, I partied harder than most. There isn't anything that I didn't do. Through those experiences, I learned that a life full of drugs, alcohol, and God knows what isn't meant for me. Ever since I realized this, I have been extremely careful of what I put in my body.

For me, my success hinges on my body's health, and if I am not going to take care of my body, nobody will. This goes true for every single person out there as well. If you aren't willing to take care of your body, you are going to miss out on so much in life.

I am not saying that you can't enjoy those little delicacies that we crave so much at times, such as cookies, but there must be a healthy counter-balance to help you retain your health at its maximum.

Personally, I love my food. This would include spinach, lean meat, and every goodness you can think of. For years, I have been working out and keeping my body as fit as it can be. In fact, I have even converted my garage into a fully functional gym.

LEAD, SERVE, WIN.

The biggest problem people face today is the fact that almost everyone is on some kind of medication. While they have all the time in the world to spend their time and money buying medicines that they believe would help them be active and healthy, they can't seem to understand just how wrong they are.

To be clear, I am all for modern medicines. One time in Tijuana, I caught something that felt like leprosy. The skin on my feet peeled off and my toenails fell out. It was brutal. I felt like I was living out the book of Job. Thankfully, all I had to do was to go to a doctor, pay $30, get my pills, and I recovered well. However, I only had to take those pills for 3 months, not for my entire life.

People, however, start using a medicine and they continue to do that perpetually. If someone recommends them an anti-depressant, they would go on to use that for as long as they can. When they do miss out on a dose, they would spend the rest of the day claiming how they are not feeling well since they have not consumed their meds.

If you are going to let medicines dictate you how your day is going to be, you are essentially losing your control over life itself. You are at the losing end, not the winning end.

This is something people need to understand. In order for you to be successful and happy at anything, you don't need a pill for that. What you need is to get out there, stay active, work on your health through all the natural ways, and conquer challenges after challenges. That's how you go out to accomplish something in life that is meaningful and joyful.

"I can't seem to study. I know, I'll take a pill for that."
"Oh, my arms are sore from the workout. I'll take a pill for that to fix that."
"I have a bad temper. An anti-depressant should help me ease up."
"I feel lost. Let's smoke up."
"I just broke up; I should drink my heart out."

    I used to do that a lot. I would smoke up or do something else to try and regain composure or kill stress somehow. While the dopamine effect did kick in, it did not change anything else. I was still facing the same problem. It was leading me nowhere. Eventually, I started realizing how this was only going on to delay my progress in life. While it did teach me lessons, I am glad that I was able to snap out of it.

    There are those who can't seem to quit at all. They are stuck with these drugs and addictions indefinitely. It is a vicious cycle that you really don't want to be a part of.

    Not so long ago, I was at Walmart. I couldn't find any potatoes. This was odd because potatoes are one thing that you can find everywhere on earth. It literally grows in dirt and I have grown it in deserts as well. Potatoes are extremely resilient that they will literally grow in your backyard if you leave them there. Therefore, it was very interesting to note that Walmart didn't have any.

Naturally, I decided to see the frozen section. Guess what? There were plenty of potatoes for everyone. All of those processed potatoes lying around in quantities you cannot fathom.

Let me clarify – I do consume processed food every now and then. I don't want to be a fear monger telling you that every microwaved meal you eat takes years off of your life. However, I feel much better when I'm eating natural whole foods, and the vast majority of my diet comes from meals I make from scratch. There are those who consume processed food as a way of life. Pop their fridge open and all you would see would be frozen food, highly-processed meals, high sugar sodas, and instant everything. They may taste nice and may even be cost-effective, but they come at the cost of your health. The more you consume these, the unhealthier your body becomes.

Just a few days ago, I had cereal. The entire day, I felt lethargic. I couldn't find that energy within me that I would normally have. It felt like a lot of work just to get out of bed and take a shower.

All I did was to have a bowl full of cereal and I felt stunted. It was clear that this wasn't something I should be consuming at all. The only reason I bought this cereal box was because I needed my carb source, since Walmart was out of potatoes.

You Are What You Eat!

Let's test this out. Let this be one more nugget for you to try and work with. For the next week, focus on consuming only fresh fruits, vegetables, grains, dairy products, lean meat, and so on. Of course, if you are allergic to something, find a healthier alternative for that. Just for the next week, change your diet.

Just a day before you start with this new diet, take notes of how you generally feel, how much energy you seem to have during the day, and other things, such as:

1. Can you maintain focus throughout the day easily?
2. Do you feel lethargic?
3. Do you have body aches?
4. Do you stress easily?
5. Is your temper controlled?
6. How anxious are you every day?

For the next week, keep track of whatever happens. By the end of the week, I assure you; you would be stunned by the difference you will find. Why such a massive difference? Simple – You can't beat natural goodness.

When you feed yourself with all the healthy food you can get, you not only become healthy from within, your mind starts functioning healthy too. With a healthy mind and body, you are then in a far better position to help yourself, your business, and the people around you. You are able to put in the kind of efforts you need to make things work, without burning yourself out almost immediately.

Being healthy is the most selfless thing you can do!

Back when I was younger, I would resort to smoking up, eating junk food, and feel all lousy and buzzed. Clearly, I had the wrong idea of being spiritual. Going to the gym, eating spinach, or do anything that was remotely healthy was something I was avoiding because I felt like I didn't need them. With time, I realized just how wrong I was. Now I lift heavy 5-6 times a week, eat my vegetables, and don't trust any pills stronger than an Advil.

What You Really Need!

When I say your body is your temple, I don't necessarily mean you should work out. That's just a part of what you should be doing.

Health is power. If your body is healthy, you are empowered to put all of your heart's dreams and all of your minds ideas into action. If you aren't healthy, you can't even lift a pen and write something down, let alone operate a business or work 9 to 5 with laser-sharp focus.

It is a problem that has been plaguing our society for a while, and the numbers continue to growing alarmingly high. Instead of choosing a lifestyle that is centered around junk food, processed food, and sugar, take a step back and change what you feed your body.

1. **Food** – Ditch those processed food items that you have been consuming all this time. Have a consistent diet to help you feel and act better.
2. **Sleep** – You need to sleep, period. Don't spend your hours watching Netflix or scrolling pointlessly through your social feeds. When it's time to rest, you rest!
3. **Sugar** – That's your enemy number one. Cut out sugar as much as possible. Trust me; you'd be thanking me later.
4. **Keep Hydrated** – Your body needs water. Instead of topping yourself up with other drinks and beverages, stick to water. It can help you remain super active and help your body to function smoothly.
5. **Workout Regularly** – Of course, I don't mean you should work out every day. You can stick to 2 days, 3 days, 4 or even 5 days of work out regime a

week. Get that blood pumping and let your muscles gain more strength. You will need all the strength you can find to help your body fight off ailments, stress, and other problems.

6. **Go Outside** – When you step outside of your house, you feel better. Being inside the house is something we have quickly grown used to. However, every once in a while, it is a good idea to step outside. Make it a daily thing to step outside, get some fresh air, may be walk a little around the block, just to regain your mental clarity and manage any stress or anxiety you may have. Furthermore, it allows you to socialize too, which can always be a bonus your way. Not only that, you will also provide your body with Vitamin D, something you can't really find elsewhere.

You cannot beat what's natural. God has created everything to help you be good, feel good, and do good with. However, it is we, the human beings, who have found disastrous alternatives. Today, we are so blinded by the sheer marketing campaigns that we can't even see the threats even if they are right in front of us. This could be that beverage you picked up, a packet of cigarettes, alcohol, drugs, medicines, or even the "Super Healthy" cereals you find on the shelves.

When it comes to the sun, we need it. Whether we like it or not, the fact is that not only does the sunshine gives our body the vital vitamin source it needs, but it really helps you function properly. You need natural light. You can install all sorts of lights within your house, but there is something about natural light and that beautiful sunshine that you cannot replicate using any known light source in the market.

Making the Shift

Of course, all of what I have just told you makes no sense unless you have a reason that compels you to take a complete 180 turn in life. They say your "why" should make you cry, meaning that you need a very strong reason why you want to change things in your life. Just stating "I want to be healthier," isn't strong enough. You must really dig deep within yourself to find out why you want to be healthy and for what purpose.

I have seen a lot of people going through tougher experiences before understanding the importance of being healthy. Then, there are those who started with their entrepreneurial journey and quickly realized how they cannot do anything unless they start taking care of their health.

Take it from someone who had experienced the disastrous results of leading an unhealthy life; you want to lead a healthy life.

LEAD, SERVE, WIN.

Back in the days, I had a girlfriend and things were well. By this time, I had already separated myself from all the partying stuff, such as recreational drugs and smoking up. However, my girlfriend somehow managed to overdose one night. It was heart-breaking to find out that she had unfortunately died because of the overdose.

Mind you, I was still consuming processed fast food, like McDonalds, and smoking cigarettes. That winter, I developed a pneumonia. As a smoker, I would still light up a cigarette but the moment I would try to inhale a cigarette, it would nearly kill me.

Had it not been for God, I would probably have died as well. I managed to recover from pneumonia somehow, and I cannot thank God enough for that.

Here's why I do believe God works in mysterious ways, especially when you are seeking His help. Just a few months later, I went back to college because I only needed one credit hour to round up everything. Since I couldn't find something that was interesting, I kept searching until I came across physical fitness.

"Oh, that seems doable."

For me, it felt like an easier subject to choose and to score that all-important credit hour. What I failed to realize back then was how God had placed me in such a position that

I had no other option but to study something that would benefit me for the rest of my life.

That class was something else. Part of the class required me to go to the gym, and that was something that would also stick with me for the rest of my life.

They would talk about protein windows, and concepts that are something nobody keeps track of anymore. Needless to say, most of what they taught was just very badly done. However, everything still stuck with me. I started keeping track of other things, such as how many reps I am doing and how I was going to refill the energy I had lost. All I had was this little notecard, which at the time seemed stupid. Today, that very same notecard serves as the basis through which I can keep track of everything.

With time, I started feeling better. While I wasn't doing much, I was at a point in life where anything I would do would be better.

What you measure gets managed!

For me, the death of my girlfriend was a wake-up call that helped me realize the importance of health. This is why I am here writing this crazy chapter so that you, the reader, can understand just how important it is for you to start working towards your health. If you have a healthy body, everything gets managed and everything gets done. However, I know

LEAD, SERVE, WIN.

that there are those who would spend every minute of the day working on their business, which is good, but they do not leave enough time to work on themselves. Such an approach will not allow you to stick around long enough.

Work is nice, but excess of everything is lethal. Too much work will get in the way of your life. It will ruin relationships, family time, isolate you from those you love, and that's just a start of it. However, if you are healthy enough, you can learn how to manage things better because you would have far more energy within you to spend time with your family instead of coming home and just crashing onto your bed.

Take a look at Kim Sinatra. She would always be doing yoga and eating a lot of veggies and ensuring she remains super healthy. She is a renowned entrepreneur and yet she never compromises on her health. That is the kind of commitment towards her health that allows her to be so successful.

This is something you would find with every single successful entrepreneur. They would always take the time out to work on their bodies and ensure they eat healthy food. While they would have their Thanksgiving turkey dinners and enjoy an occasional drink or two, they would never compromise on their health. They would ensure they always prioritize their health because if they are healthy, so is their life.

The Takeaway

Your body is what allows you to move, to do things you want to, and to think clearly. If you feed your body with all the wrong stuff, you will cloud your judgment, disturb the natural balance of chemicals and hormones, and that can lead to catastrophic results.

Our bodies are a gift to us by God. If we do not take care of them, we will be answerable for that later on. Whether you are obese or underweight, you can change everything about you and your life. All it needs is grit, resiliency, and commitment to yourself.

Here are some tips to get you started in the right direction:

1. Start eating healthy
2. Keep yourself hydrated
3. Exercise
4. Avoid drugs, medications, and alcohol
5. Stop smoking
6. Rest

This chapter was meant to help you understand how everything revolves around your health. Therefore, the lessons to take away are:

LEAD, SERVE, WIN.

1. Your success as a leader depends on your health.
2. It's easier to add a healthy habit than to quit an unhealthy one.
3. If you really care about yourself, you'll probably have to quit those unhealthy habits too.

Write: What is one healthy habit that I'm willing to start?

Chapter 5

To Thine Own Self, Be True

    A lot of people not really understand just important it is to acknowledge their actions. Instead of taking responsibility and being honest to themselves, they find ways to rationalize their decisions and actions. Owing to this, they often end up compromising on a lot of the little stuff and think, "Ah! It's not going to harm." However, you compromise once, for whatever reason, rest assured that it will come back to haunt you later.

    "I only took a pill because I didn't sleep well last night."

    No, sir! You took that pill because you couldn't really overcome the urge to take the pill. You have been through a lot of sleepless nights and have fared just as good the other day.

Our mind continues to find reasons to connect the dots with. This is how things work, but that doesn't mean we cannot reprogram or rewire our mindset. We can, and we will!

The point I am trying to make here is simple; stop compromising. In the case of our friend who took the pill because they couldn't get a good night's sleep, the obvious solution was to work on their sleep habits instead of popping pills. They may have taken just a single pill today, but the immediate effects would then lure them to take another the next day "Because it felt good." Before you know it, they would be struggling with side-effects and an addiction to the pill.

Stop Doing What Everyone is Doing

Jordan Peterson explains that every person has two voices inside. One of the voices tells you to go while the other one tells you to stop. Only one voice can win, and you get to decide which one that is. The more you listen to a specific voice, the stronger it becomes.

We see this almost every day. Most of the people who started smoking did so because they saw others doing it and thought, "Well, everybody's doing it…" And that opened a floodgate of problems and addiction.

We also see this in a professional setting where you know you want to quit the job and either start your own business or find another one. However, you tell yourself, "I will quit this job, but I will work for just one more year and get it sorted."

Not long after, you decided to buy a house because everyone's buying one too, not because you are ready to make such a move. As a result, you go through the process, take a massive loan, and are now left to make repayments for years to come.

With each of these compromises, you are deviating from your goals. You are losing track of what you were supposed to do and end up with something completely different. The bad news is that you can't undo what you have already done. You cannot bring back time that has been lost. Once gone, it's gone for good.

When you are following what everyone's doing, you are not really working towards your legacy; you are working towards pieces of legacies that others are aiming for. In the end, you are left with a life that you lived and will have nothing to be remembered by. Why? You would have done just what everybody would have done; nothing special, nothing worth remembering. That can change though, and only you can do that.

The problem is that most people do not align their legacies with God. Most of the people are far more focused on "What does God have for me," as opposed to "What am I doing for God?"

LEAD, SERVE, WIN.

I know that I do not need to be the main character in the universe – That task was done perfectly well by Jesus. However, this does not mean that I have no role at all. When you set your goals and you work towards it, you can then work towards your legacy. On the other hand, if you betray yourself, in any shape or form, the only person that is going to be hurt at the end of the day is you. Nobody else would feel an iota of a difference.

Being dishonest to yourself is something most of us do without even realizing it. You may not want to do something but you are doing it anyway because you have rationalized to yourself that you need to do this in order to move ahead in life. Take a leaf from the book of entrepreneurship. The entrepreneurs would never do something they know they aren't supposed to do or something that they don't want to do. This may mean that they are throwing a multi-million-dollar opportunity out of the window, but that's okay. Why? Because it isn't them. Instead, they would focus on creating their own legacy. They know what they aim for and align everything they do accordingly. As a result, they only go on to achieve the kind of results most of us can only dream of.

Of course, I am not saying that you shouldn't buy insurance, buy a house, a car, because that is something you need. However, this isn't what you were put on earth to do. These are things you can work for, but what about after you have achieved them? Does your purpose to exist ends here? It doesn't.

This is where people tend to lose the most. Just because they may have worked hard for a day that they can take tomorrow a bit easier. When you start taking things easy, what you are essentially doing is lying to yourself. Today was different, and tomorrow is going to be something else altogether. If you start taking things lightly, you may end up going backwards in life, not forwards.

Becoming True to Myself

The day I decided that I was going to move to Florida from Vegas was when I really started becoming true to myself. As it happens, my mother had moved around a year or so before I did. However, the weather here meant that her health deteriorated quickly. She ended up getting breast cancer, but she ended up winning the battle comfortably. When we thought that things were not going to get any worse, she ended up getting a very severe form of Alzheimer's disease. This meant that she needed attention 24 hours a day.

Whenever I would have vacations, I would come in to spend time with my mother and ensure I took care of her. After a while, it occurred to me; why not stay here, full stop? Not only would I be able to be with my mom round the clock, but it would help me save a lot of trouble every month because then, I wouldn't have to fly out to meet her after every 4 weeks.

"That's it then. I am moving to Florida."

At this point, I was working from home. The only problem with this plan was the fact that I really didn't like to ask for permission to work. Since we were working from home, it meant I had to do my routine work activities facing a laptop while being inside a house. That part was okay, but asking to see if I could move to Florida was something that wasn't sitting well with me.

Of course, I always had the option to quit but that would have meant to restart all over again, and time wasn't exactly a luxury I had at this point.

Mind you, Nevada was getting bad anyway. Even if it wasn't for my mom, I might have moved out somewhere else sooner or later. Like most entrepreneurs, I cannot imagine myself being tied up in a position where I have to ask permission to get my job done. Despite having a good upward trajectory and tons of job security, I knew I had to break away from these chains.

It wasn't just people either. Nevada was becoming more like California. So many rules came in, such as HOV lanes and wearing masks in grocery stores. It was no longer the Wild West Vegas that I had grown to love. The idea that I needed permission in order to drive on a specific lane or that I was restricted from it bothered me a lot. Living there was getting bad.

Nevada was going downhill fast, and I had to get out of there in time so that I could be closer to my family and lead the kind of life I wanted to.

When you have a strong purpose and a strong sense of direction in life, you automatically start picking up signals the minute your life starts going off-course. When things start changing or they start impacting you, you will start finding ways to resume your life on the track you want it to be on. Whether that means you need to quit your job and find another one, move out of the city or even the state, you will do it. Why? Because you are now being honest to yourself.

Do you want people to follow you into battle? First, you must be honest with yourself all the way. Others can tell when something doesn't add up.

The Takeaway

A lot of people think they know what they want in life, but then they go on to compromise on so many fronts. The more you compromise in life, the further away you deviate yourself from the goal. To you, it may just be a one-time thing and you might think, "It wouldn't hurt." However, every time you compromise over something, it comes bearing a cost.

LEAD, SERVE, WIN.

For me, the idea of moving to Florida made more sense, but it would have meant for me to find a place for myself and adjust to the new settings. However, I could have chosen to stick to Vegas, and that would have been me compromising on my goals and aims. The cost? I would need permission to do what I wanted to do, and that isn't something I am willing to compromise on.

It took me a while to find clarity in life, but once there, I have never done anything that isn't true to my nature, in line with my goals, or that contradicts my beliefs. Whatever set of goals you may have, be sure to align all your decisions to those goals. If you are a leader, you likely got distracted by somebody else's vision along the way. It's great to help others – in fact, it is essential – but they are responsible for carrying out their vision, and you are responsible for yours. You do not want to deviate from your goal because it would take time for you to get back on track, and time is a luxury nobody has. Once time goes by, you can't bring it back.

Write: What has distracted you from your dreams?

Chapter 6

Delegate the Details

Here's a statement that will get you kicked out of most corporate job interview: I don't like paying too much attention to minute details. It's not that I can't; it's simply that if I was to spend all my time on every little thing, I would end up wasting time I could have been directing the bigger picture.

Entrepreneurs need to value their time more than anything. This naturally means that we will never let our time be wasted doing something somebody else can do better, as well, or even just good enough. By wasting our time, I do not mean partying or doing anything that isn't work related. I've done plenty of that in my late teens and early twenties. I'm talking about wasting time doing things that look like being responsible on the surface: accounting, taking inventory of things, calling clients, setting up meetings, scheduling meetups. I am supposed to work on the business, not in it. This means that if I am not interested in these tasks, I would rather have someone else hired for this job that is. As a result, I would end up freeing up my time and that would allow me to focus on what I do best for the business. At the same time, someone else that I would hire, I know that they would be able to handle the aspects far more effectively than I could.

    Back when I was working 60 or even 70 hours a week at Tim's Tutors, my time was at such a premium that I needed to get creative to buy it back. I had a woman named Christine that I would pay to pick up my groceries, clean my house twice a week, and I had another girl named Ashley who would drive me to client appointments, to the school I was teaching at, and even to the gym at five in the morning. This team was there to ensure I didn't waste my time in doing things that I knew were either not rewarding enough for my time or were something I just wanted to avoid altogether. There were many mornings when I would have skipped the gym if Ashley wasn't waiting for me at oh dark thirty to get the day started – plus, since I didn't need to keep my eyes on the road, I was able to take care of all my emails and social media in the car instead of saving them for when I got home. This is how I turned 70 hour scatterbrained weeks into 50 hour focused weeks.

    Think about it for a minute; if your hourly worth is $200, would you want to spend an hour washing your car or doing the lawn, or would you prefer to make $200 or more in the same time and let someone else take over the little tasks? Obviously, you would prefer the latter. Yes, you may have to pay this person like $50, but you are still saving $150 as a result. Had it been you doing these chores, you would have lost every penny of that $200 that you could have made but chose not to. Chris saved me thousands of dollars just by going to the grocery store – this was before grocery delivery became widespread, plus she knew to pick the freshest vegetables – not to mention, coming home to a clean house with a fully stocked fridge did wonders for my mental health.

Entrepreneurs work the same way. They are always working on their strengths while delegating everything else away. They can outsource these tasks to virtual assistants, or they can hire someone to come in and do those tasks for them. As a result, they are truly able to gain the freedom they need to work on the business, not in it.

Outsourcing – License to Freedom

Back in the early days of Tim's Tutors, I would post a lot of posts on social media, run ad campaigns all over the place, and most of my time would go there. However, whenever I would come home, I would still continue doing that because I wasn't finished for the day. All that driving around, going to the grocery stores, going shopping, it wasted my time. This meant that I would always bring my work to home, and that is something you really don't want to do.

What's the point? If I cannot free up enough of my time to spend it with my family, I was clearly doing something wrong. Therefore, it made perfect sense that I should hire someone that could help me do my groceries for me. CHECK. It made sense to hire someone that could drive me around so that I could continue posting while I was being taken from point "A" to point "B." CHECK. Similarly, I had someone come over and clean the house twice a week. This would save me hours of time, allowing me to continue focusing on work that I do best. They walk away with their wages, I would spend my time productively, everybody wins.

What I did was to buy back time for myself. While I would have loved to delegate reading my emails, that's a part that I can't. The fact is that some of these emails are confidential. These may contain private information of my clients, sensitive material that must not be shared with others, such as business plans, financial numbers, and so on. Freeing up my time, therefore, allowed me to ensure I could have enough time to go through each one of these without feeling like I should hurry up and move on to the next one due to time constraints.

Before You Outsource...

Now, a lot of you may rush towards delegating almost everything you can think of, just so you can kick back and relax. That is neither the point of delegating and outsourcing your tasks, nor is it the goal.

Outsourcing is a tool. If you know what you're doing, you can build something great with it. If you aren't careful, you can hurt yourself and those around you. How many leaders read "The Four Hour Workweek" by a different Tim, and began to think that laziness was a goal in itself. I don't think that was the goal of that book, but I know a lot of people who started the automation without the planning, and ended up making their lives more complicated. A lot of the people I know would have absolutely no idea what they should outsource and what they shouldn't. To help them, here are a few tips worth taking into consideration. These will help you understand what aspects of your life or business you can outsource.

Know What's Productive

Knowing your strengths allows you to know what you should keep doing yourself. In most of the cases, these strengths are generally what your business is centered around. If you are an extroverted people person, you should free up as much time as possible to spend time in social situations that will grow your business. This will let you attract more clients, grow a network, and find more lucrative opportunities within your network. If you are good with math and spreadsheets, you may want to stay behind the scenes crunching numbers, and let your team be the face of your business. If you're uncomfortable on the phone, there is no point in you making cold calls all day. This will drain the energy you could be spending on your strengths, and it would be far better to have a specialist handle that part for you.

You should also be able to know how much your hourly net worth really is. If you work 8 hours a day, and take a break for around 2 hours, you only need to account for those 6 hours. Therefore, divide your month's average net earnings by the number of days you work, and divide that further by 6 hours to find out what your hourly net worth is.

Once you know this, you would be able to know what's actually productive and what isn't. Now, meeting new clients can allow you to do more business. However, look at the number of hours you spend against the returns that you get. Is it more or less than your hourly net worth? If it is more, you can stick with that. If it is less, delegate that to someone else. Similarly, making a cold-call may fetch you a lead, but that lead comes after 10 calls. On average, a call will take 2 minutes, so that is roughly around 20 minutes of work. For every cold lead that turns warm, you will then need to close them and acquire their business. This process may take another 30 minutes to an hour (as an example). If what you make after the lead is converted and closed properly is less (which it will most likely be), you need to delegate this part to someone else.

Do not waste your time in doing tasks that cannot generate you the amount of money you are worth. This is why outsourcing is a better alternative for every entrepreneur. Not only does that help them save time, but it also allows them to create jobs for others. You continue growing your business your way, and your employees will continue pitching towards your goals of the business at the same time.

Keep Doing the Work You Love

In most cases, if you like doing something, you are probably good at it. In my case, not only did I delegate a lot of business tasks to others, but I also hired people that would clean my house for me, drive me around, and do groceries for me. However, there is one household chore that I refused to delegate: cooking.

I love making food, and I still continue to create my own recipes. Chopping the onions, finding the perfect blend of spices, and firing up the grill is a form of meditation to me. I do have a strange habit of doing the dishes at someone else's house if I see a pile of dishes there, but I'm glad I have Chris to clean up in my kitchen.

This may sound weird, but that's just me. All of us are wired in a different way. However, what unites us together under a single flag is the fact that we are all visionaries.

Delegating Isn't Spending – It's Investing

Entrepreneurs, by the words' very definition, are known to have their visions and the ability to do what it takes to pursue those visions. However, a lot of entrepreneurs tend to go wrong when they start doing everything on their own. When you do that, your mind isn't as focused as it should be. Therefore, your attention is divided and so are your efforts. As a result, you cannot achieve any meaningful result.

Jack of all trades, master of none!

There are those who would much rather do everything on their own because they really do not want to pay anyone else handling their tasks. To them, "I would make more money by not hiring anyone." Well, don't be surprised when you don't actually make enough money at all.

Stop looking at paying someone as an expense. If anything, it is actually you buying yourself time. While I don't expect you to change your mindset right away, I do expect you to let this sink in. Take inventory of everything and understand how paying someone could free up your time, how much of it, and how you can better use that time to create more ways to earn revenue.

We have this tendency of not thinking outside the box, even though we love to think that we do. Most of us have absolutely no idea what to delegate, if to delegate anything. To me, when I delegated the driving aspect of my day-to-day routine, it was a light-bulb moment.

Road rage is real: I remember many mornings stuck in the all-day rush hour that is Las Vegas traffic. I'm pretty resilient, but I do get stressed out and distracted when I feel stuck. Instead of dodging drunk tourists, I was utilizing that time to do more social posting. I was being more efficient.

Of course being dropped off and picked up from the school led to rumors that I was the one with the penchant for drunk driving, even though I don't drink alcohol at all. The teachers I was close to all told me they were jealous of my lifestyle. The fact is, it does feel luxurious to have someone on call – unlike a random taxi or Uber, Ashley knew my routine to the minute, and my favorite snacks. Having someone on YOUR team empowers them to go above and beyond. The Navy taught me that early is on-time and on-time is late, but sometimes traffic can be a force of nature. If I was ever running behind schedule, Ashley knew to reach out to my clients and give them an updated ETA. This made my clients feel luxurious too.

Building people up is what I do. I can't delegate what I do best to someone else. Instead, I started with the things that hate the most and other smaller things, and I started delegating them to someone else. As a result, I ended up freeing a significant part of my time. That was what allowed me to continue doing what I do best. As a result, I was drawing in more clients, generating far more revenue, and was able to build up thousands of students and hundreds of team members.

I wish more teachers would go into Human Resources. Good teachers know how to identify talent and get the best out of students. If companies would invest in their people the way the best teachers invest in their students, we would have legions of workers obsessed with their founders' missions. If building people up is not the number one skillset and gift of a founder, they need to delegate team-building to someone who can build people up and focus those people on the founder's mission.

The Subtle Patterns

I know a lot of entrepreneurs who love marketing. They tend to be masters of one specific piece of the marketing puzzle. However, being good at marketing is like being good at "computers." A brilliant network engineer might be a terrible coder. A founder might be great at putting their vision into words, but terrible at making content visually appealing or automating their email campaigns: best hire someone that can help them fill that gap for them. I personally love going on Facebook live and interacting with my community, because it aligns perfectly with my gifting of getting to know people and building them up. I'm absolutely terrible with graphic design. Which aspect of marketing I handle personally, and which aspect I delegate? Don't fall into the trap that the only part of marketing you need is the part you enjoy, and don't be afraid to delegate according to your specific strengths and weaknesses.

Do not go on and delegate things haphazardly. You might end up hiring more people than you may be able to manage. The best way to find out what needs to be delegated right away and what must be retained is to get your feet wet. With time, you will be able to see a pattern emerging. You might just realize that all that you are delegating pertains to marketing. In this case, you can take an informed decision and hire a marketing specialist. It could be anything, but in order for it to work for you, you need to experience things and find out what you need to delegate. Figure out the pattern and then take actions accordingly.

There will come a point where you would be managing a lot of people, a lot of teams, and that's where you will need to delegate aspects that are unproductive in nature to you. Instead of talking to all these people, you can have just one person acting as the manager that reports to you. As a result, you don't have to talk to everyone; you just talk to this person and that's that.

When it comes to HR and recruiting, entrepreneurs tend to keep pretty close to the chests. However, just because they do it does not mean you should do the same. If that's something you can't do or be bothered with, let someone else take over. Remember, we do not do what everyone is doing; we forge our own ways.

HR is essential, but it has become synonymous with the red-tape that has spurred so many entrepreneurs to quit their corporate jobs and take a risk on themselves. While its purpose is quite literally to dig for gold, find the best of the best, most of them don't really do that anymore. A lot of firms are now switching to software-based HR solutions – Ironical, isn't it? It's meant to be "Human" resources, not "Software" resources.

When you settle for software, it will end up auto-rejecting a lot of potential gold. These are the people that could take your business to the next level. Software is a tool – an incredibly useful tool – but if you dehumanize your recruiting process, you're going to have a hard time getting the people who make it through that process to care about your company. Your recruiting process is your first opportunity to make an impression on the people you are going to trust with your mission.

When I was building Prep Expert's team of world-class educators for Mark Cuban and Shaan Patel as their Director of Academics, we got hundreds of thousands of applications for instructor and tutoring roles. How did I cut through the noise? Engagement! Since we were looking for people with top SAT scores, I created a template in Indeed asking for them to email me their score reports as a file attachment. I then created a workflow where our Operations Manager would make sure this template got sent to every single person who applied for these positions through an automated process: this is how you incorporate software. Do you know how many of those hundreds of thousands of applicants ever sent the requested PDFs? Less than one percent. This is how I cut through the noise, and still showed every applicant the respect of a human interaction. I personally monitored the special inbox that we had them email their score reports to. Do you know how many emails in that inbox included the required file attachment? Again, less than one percent. Every single person who followed through on sending their qualifying test scores got a personal message from me congratulating them on making it to the top 1% of the top 1% of our hiring process, and it barely took any time out of my day. What's more important is that these candidates became even more excited about joining our team than when they first applied. Does your company's hiring process do this?

<u>The Takeaway</u>

Delegating things is okay, but delegate the right stuff. In designing the hiring funnel for Prep Expert I delegated to another human (my ops manager), a process (the template and workflow), and software (the Indeed platform and automation bots), but I always maintained control of the process, and kept a personal touch to build an enthusiastic team that cared about our mission. To help you become a better delegator, I talked about:

1. Figuring out what to delegate
2. Knowing what's productive and what isn't
3. Figure out the pattern

From there, it is all about seeing the results. If the results are good, continue the process. If you need to pivot a little, it's okay as well. For those who will work for you, if they are doing a good job and the numbers are there to prove that, give them a raise or a promotion. Do not wait because the longer you wait, the likelier they are to leave the job.

TIM PRUNYI

Write: What is one thing you hate doing and are willing to delegate?

Chapter 7

Don't Delegate the Vision

In the previous chapter, we learned how delegating all the mundane tasks because they weigh you down, burden you, and slow the pace of your progress is okay. In this chapter, however, we will learn what you NEVER should delegate – Your vision.

Your vision needs to be your baby. You need to care about it, or nobody else will. Whatever business model you are working with, whatever progress you have made thus far, and whatever you may plan for the future, only you can pursue that. There is not another soul on this earth that can share your vision 100% and pursue it for you. There is not a single human being out there that can act as your clone, have the same thought process, prioritize the same things in life, work towards the same goals and act according to the same principles as you. You are unique, and so is your vision.

Learning My Lesson

Back when I was teaching at Tim's Tutors, I learned this lesson, and I am glad I did. Tim's Tutors was a teaching business where we would help kids learn English, Math, and what have you. If someone needed to improve their grammar, I would need someone that would know grammar in the first place. If someone needed help with their math concepts, I needed someone who was good at mathematics. I couldn't just send anybody to do these jobs.

My initial success actually came by breaking the so-called status-quo that existed. To begin with, there were so many rules that were involved in the teaching business. I chose to break most of them. I did that by literally bringing in a new way to teach kids, how to present the material that was to be taught, and this may not have sat well with any of your usual teachers out there.

With time, I realized that there were things that weren't working for me. Naturally, I delegated those aspects of the school. As more time went on, it became apparent that me delegating those aspects of the business didn't really do anything. If anything, those aspects were going further back.

Mind you, these are the aspects that I really had to work on because they were the reason, or lack of them, that pushed children to find tutors in the first place.

I wish I had figured this part out earlier, but it took me quite some time to actually figure out that some things were not going right.

With time, I started receiving text messages from parents, requesting me to meet them in person. They would tell me how their math tutor or their grammar tutor wasn't up to the mark, and that hit me by surprise. On paper, these were some of the best people for the job, and yet, there I was being peppered with concerns and worries. I had to do something, and the best way for me was to focus on my people, just so I could see what they were doing wrong.

As it turns out, these "best" of the people were actually teaching the kids exactly how they were being taught in the school. Remember, I had already gone the other direction because I knew just how bad the schools would generally teach.

"Look. We need to retrace our steps here. I see that you are teaching these children just as any other school would, but that didn't work for them."

I would then start explaining how we are trying to teach them differently so that the children could actually learn and grow their knowledge.

TIM PRUNYI

The problem why that happened was simple – I wasn't at the driving seat. When you have a vision and you are not the one in control, that vehicle will go in all sorts of different directions. In the end, you would either need to jump back in the driver's seat or just walk away completely. To me, shutting the entire business down was never an option, therefore, I decided to jump back in and recast the vision.

If it was just me, I would never need to say it out loud because my vision would be in my head, in my heart, and in my thoughts all the time. However, it wasn't just me now. I had many others who were working for me. In order to bring them all on a single page, to align their efforts in line with my vision, I had to step in and talk to them. They needed to know what my vision was and what I expect them to do.

It is only natural that when you bring new people, you feel like they are the right people for the job because they share the same vision as you. That's a mistake. There is a reason why many successful entrepreneurs put many of their candidates through personality tests, training, and then explain to them what the vision is. They want to make sure that everyone is on board and that everyone knows what role they are playing, how it feeds into the vision, and how their efforts create progress.

"Look. Our purpose is quite simple – We go against everything you might have learned in school. You may have taught your whole career, but this is where it must change. My vision is to teach in the most productive manner so that the students truly learn."

Since then, I had always ensured that every new candidate knows what we are aiming for. This was particularly useful when retired teachers approached us.

We would inform them of how we were aiming to do things very differently and then leave it up to them to decide if they were up for the job or if they would prefer applying elsewhere. Either way, they would know what the vision was, and they would know what they would be expected to do.

Building a team means you need to get really comfortable sharing your vision on a regular basis. You can always record a video – or write a book – to preserve your message, but you still need to communicate this regularly. People forget quickly! Tim's Tutors was a success because I came back in and shared my vision with everyone from top to bottom. My vision is something I knew best. While I didn't realize just how important it was for me to maintain control over my vision, I do now, thanks to that experience.

Cast Your Vision

I know, a lot of you might be wondering how I would share my vision and shape it in a way that everyone understands.

When it comes to the business, I try to be as specific as possible. If I was to say "I want my business to grow," it would be vague, ambiguous, and won't really click with anyone. However, if I was to say "I want my business to earn $1 million this year," it would then be super specific.

For my tutoring business, however, my vision had to be very student-centric. Remember, my entire purpose for the business was to help students learn, not make money out of them. If my vision was to make money, I would have done a million different things and probably made significant returns. Instead, my vision was to be someone the students and their parents could trust and rely on to teach in the most effective manner possible.

You can actually generalize this for any business. Instead of being student-centric, you would aim for a client-centric approach where you would put the needs of the clients first before your own. That's a recipe for success. Now, whenever you start formulating your strategies, you would always go for things that would go on to benefit the client the most.

For me, it was never about my reputation in the industry. It was never about the money either. It was always about the student and the experience they get by choosing my team of tutors. It was all about helping them excel and improve their grades so that they could go on and help someone else later on in life.

Consistency is Key

I had a great onboarding presentation in the start that was pretty clear. Then, about six to nine months in, people would start fading out of the vision and fall back to their older ways of teaching. This was particularly applicable to those who worked part-time. This was a problem because I needed consistency. I didn't want to be known for being a tutoring business that works best in certain months and sucks for the rest of the year. I needed consistency. I wanted Tim' Tutors to be the best choice for students, period.

In order to have consistency, you need to bring in reminders. Personally, I would recommend that you carry out a team meeting or something that would remind everyone of the actual goals and vision of the company every week. You can go through the performances of all your workers and analyze if they are moving in the right direction. If they are, appreciate them. If they aren't, talk to them and remind them of what you stand for and what you expect them to do. If they are still unable to deliver, do not wait that long. Hire fast, fire faster.

When you have a reminder every week, it helps them on some level to raise their motivation and reset their energy levels to 100%. It helps them know what they need to focus on for the rest of the week in order to ace it. The more specific and clear you explain your vision or goals, the easier it would be for them to carry the actions out.

So, how do you remind them every week? Well, I can think of a few ways:

1. Weekly meeting – Mind you, this can get fussy really quickly
2. Text messages
3. Emails
4. Announcements

When you have the entire team aligned towards the same goal, and all of you work in the same direction, the output can be far more impressive than you might imagine. Of course, this does mean that you may have to pivot a bit every now and then. I know that because I know I may have to pivot from time to time as well.

I remember how I used to loathe common core maths and thought it was a perfect rip off as it never really provided any value to the student. With time, I realized I couldn't just tell my students to show the finger to it and say "It's pointless." I had to find workarounds, and I did. Ironically, a lot of states are now pulling away from teaching common core mathematics to students, and that is just music to my ears!

I would much rather have the child learn two methods to solve a problem and then be at liberty to choose which method they found better. It worked and it really helped students realize that there are other ways to solve the same problem; they just need to search for those solutions.

There are those who would cast their vision just once and believe that it would suffice. They would believe that it would be sufficient for everyone and that everyone would then work perpetually towards that vision. That has always led to serious consequences.

Vision Statements

The fact is that we live in a world that continues to evolve faster than most can keep pace with. Therefore, recalling and recasting the vision not only ensures everyone knows what they must do and what they shouldn't, but it also serves as a perfect way to find out if the vision needs to be tweaked or not.

Think about it; Tim's Tutors would have focused on in-person tutoring for life had COVID not hit. After the lockdowns, the only way a kid would learn was through Zoom or other online mediums. While the vision mostly remained the same, it was just tweaked so that it could continue to work and apply necessary changes.

For most companies, it is just a box to check. They believe they need a mission statement, and for that, they would just Google one out and be done with it. Then, people would use fluff and wordy sentences to make it sound good, but does it actually work? No, it doesn't.

"We are here to ensure we serve our environment in the best way possible by minimizing carbon emissions." Remind me, what do you do? Coal mining? That's VERY environment-friendly!

If you are trying to use these words as your vision, you are either in the wrong field, or you are just not too sure what you are aiming for. Either way, you need to know what you are aiming for, what you intend to do, and how you will do that.

In case of an education business, your vision statement shouldn't be too far from having something to do with students and the education itself. Do not stray off on a tangent just because you wanted the statement to be flamboyant, elaborate, and worth the praise. You aren't there for the praises though; you're there to deliver a service.

The easier your vision statement and mission statement are, the easier it would be to modify these with time.

If It Isn't Fun, It's Not Okay

Your core values are your own. Based on those core values, you set up your vision, your goals, and essentially the entire business itself. However, when you let someone else take over the driving seat, they would come with their own set of unique core values. There will be a clear clash of interest and that can potentially result in the firm derailing a bit or significantly from the goals.

My business went through such a phase only when I decided to take a step back and let others drive my business. Clearly, it was not heading in the direction I wanted it to go. Where my focus was to be different and to teach more effectively, things were returning back to the regular "Okay, let's get your grades up" kind of a deal. Sure, you can get the grades up, but what's the point if the student never truly understood the concepts properly? It's neither fun nor productive. Our job is not to teach how to cram everything; it is to understand and get deep into the concept.

Speaking of fun, a lot of people have made their lives more miserable because they are missing out on the essential fun aspect of life. If your job is something that is fun and makes you feel good, the hours would go by instantly. However, when you are doing something that involves no fun, it immediately becomes a lot more serious. Soon, every minute would feel like an hour, and an hour would feel like an eternity. That's not how you work. That's not you being productive.

"I don't want to go to the movies. I am working."
"I can't go to the movies. I am working."

Pretty much the same statements, right? If you pay close attention to how they were delivered, there is a difference. The first one is a person choosing not to go because they are enjoying their work. You don't get to see that every day, but it does happen. The second, however, is the usual "I can't or my boss would kill me" approach.

It is through having a strong vision that you can cut through the distractions and focus purely on work itself. Besides, if you are setting down the right vision, following the right path, and doing things right, you will actually enjoy your work. Why? Because everything you would do would fall perfectly in alignment with your own core values, goals, and vision. That's how important vision is, and that's why you really don't want to delegate that!

The Takeaway

Previously, we learned what we should aim to delegate. Here, we learned:

1. Never to delegate your vision
2. How I learned my lesson
3. Cast your vision – Remind everyone
4. Make it fun

Write: What is a mission and vision you can commit to?

Chapter 8

Stand Up for Others

To be a leader, you must know how to stand up for others and leader them. As a leader, you will have people who will be relying heavily on you.

In the corporate world, I am positioned right in the middle. This means that I get to experience a lot of things that I simply find disturbing.

There are instances where if someone ends up making a simple human error, they would be facing consequences that are just downright unjustifiable.

Why Should You Stand Up for Your People?

If someone happens to be teaching a class of 100 kids, there is a possibility that some parents may not like the way this person is teaching. They would talk about how they didn't like the shirt the teacher wore, how he explained some concepts, or how they stumbled on a question. These parents tend to forget that teachers aren't robots; they are human beings. We are bound to run into some mistakes or errors every now and then.

Add to that the fact that this person is teaching a class with numerous students present at the same time. If all of them start asking questions at the same time, that person would never be able to answer all of them at once.

I know how my people take a lot of slack and abuse. Being who I am, my job is to protect them to a certain extent. However, there would always come moments where we may end up getting a few complains stating that the teacher isn't their favorite teacher. They may not be, but if I see them doing their best, I am going to stand up for them whether the company likes it or not. I am there to ensure fairness and to protect the interests of my people. If they are delivering their best, they can count on me to have their backs.

People believe that because someone is a "teacher" that they would know everything. That's not the case. While they may be brilliant in their subjects, they will still need training. A lot of companies don't really put in the efforts to train their teachers and staff accordingly, meaning that when the time to comes to deliver results, the teachers find themselves ill-equipped with people skills or communication skills. That part comes down on the company, not the teacher. They still know what they need to know, but the rest happens to be the responsibility of the firm. They are supposed to train their teachers and their employees on how to develop their interpersonal skills.

Now, the most popular approach would be to have a trainer walk in, introduce themselves, play a YouTube video, ask a few questions and walk out – Training done! Who are we kidding? That's not training. To truly train the people, you need to bring in the human elements. You need to walk them through all the scenarios one by one.

Sure, if you were aiming to teach some technical skills, such as programming, a video would do nicely. However, for other skills, you need to have a trainer that can put in the hours and days to fully help the employees prepare themselves for what's about to come next.

When you have 100 teenagers on a zoom call, and most of them not actually paying much attention or making noises to distract others, how would you imagine that going? If you aren't going to put in the time to train your teachers, you are going to face a lot of backlash. What would you do then? Fire the teacher? That would be wrong. Instead, stand up for them. Understand that they are doing the best they can. If you see any room for improvement, train them better.

A Leader Must Always Have Their Back

"Workers don't owe you loyalty; they owe you performance!"

Peter Drucker

While that may be so, the fact is that when you start treating people like people, you will also start earning their loyalty. It is a no-brainer that when you treat them as human beings and are there for them in their time of need, they will come in happily to go the extra mile.

This relationship that you form with your employees is a give-take relationship. You give respect, you gain respect. You treat them right, they will do right by you. If you stand up for them, they will stand up for you as well. The same goes for your clients as well. When your client knows that you have their back, they are going to trust you and remain loyal to you. As a leader, this pivotal role comes down on your shoulders. It is up to you to lead by an example and set the right expectations. However, at the same time, you want to make sure that you have their backs and that they know you do. Once, I remember working with my former students, who were now working for me. There was this elderly teacher who was constantly talking down to them in a way that was disrespectful and quite hurtful to hear. I had to interfere and draw a line in the sand:

Don't talk to kids like that, period. Consider this a warning."

Regardless of your position, you need to learn how to stand up for people. Stand up for human beings, whether employees, clients, shareholders, or interns. This only goes to show just how strong your core values are. This is how you set precedence in the firm.

I once stood up for my boss because the contractors were quite visibly taking advantage of him. I had to intervene and straighten things up for my boss.

"Principles before personalities."

Bill Wilson

Dr. Joe Dispenza says, "Your personality creates your personal reality." That is true. The stronger your character is, the better your personal reality shapes up to be.

When you are standing firm on your principles, you will eventually start attracting all the right personalities that fit that description. You will start putting together a team of people that follow the same set of principles and core values. If you get a lot of things coming your way from people that are far too busy being negative, know that they are not aligned with your vision or are not the right fit. Don't worry – Keep stepping forward. You will find people that are worth hanging on to.

The Takeaway

Standing up to the people that work for you allows you to let the world know that you and your team are there to help each other out. It keeps the negativity outside while allowing you to focus purely on results.

You are a human being, and so are they. Treat them as such.

Be clear on your principles because a good set of principles is what defines a personality. Having principles in place and working in line with those principles, you will start acting more like a magnet that would attract similar people, and just like the saying goes "Like attracts like," you will start attracting all the right people.

By standing up for others, you are serving them!

Write: Was there ever a time you wanted to stand up for someone, but decided not to? Why?

Chapter 9

Speak Truth to Power

When you are trying to create a culture within your firm that rewards those who go the extra mile, think out of the box, and help the firm progress, you need to add one more important principle to the mix – Speaking the Truth.

It is a power that many have never fully realized but those who do, they have gone on to rewrite the pages of history.

While everyone believes speaking the truth isn't as bad, it can often be quite challenging, especially if you have clients that are clearly not a good fit for the business. Calling them and letting them know you do not wish to conduct further business activities with them is something most people get cold feet about.

The Pareto principle states that 80% of your revenue is going to come from the 20% clients you have. That's perfectly understandable, but what if one of those 20% of the clients happens to be toxic, what then?

While you can try and bend the rules a little and help them get a good experience, the fact is that there will be a point in time where you would simply want to call everything off.

If you are facing a hard client, they would quite literally nag you in the middle of the night through numerous texts and calls. They would consistently cause you headaches. They would constantly reschedule things, cancelling them, taking information about everything but never really doing anything else. All of that can quickly get hard to handle.

Now, I know you might think that the customer is always right and that we should be client-centric, and I agree. The entire idea is to be a servant to your client. However, there is a line in the sand that must be drawn. You should know what you can do and what you can't do. While you might state all of this in some email or contract, it is fairly easy for the customer to ignore that and start causing you problems.

Here's the thing; since this one client might just be one-fifth of your clients or even half of the clientele you have, would you be willing to walk away for the sake of your principles? Or, would you rather prefer to hang in there and hope that things change? Judging from my own experience, waiting will get you nowhere.

If you recall, I talked about how you should not compromise on your principles and goals. If you were to bend a little for one client, word would spread. Next, everyone would expect you to bend the rules slightly, and that would quickly turn into a disaster. For the sake of your principles, for the sake of your employees, and for your vision, let them go. The world is full of people that need your help, that need your services. Centering your entire business around a single client or spending most of your time and resources to satisfy a single client does not add up.

Look On the Bright Side

Just a few days ago, I was on the phone with my friend John, who also happens to be a mentor for a long time. He told me how his partner is pulling out of a multi-million-dollar business that both of them have operated for a while.
I remember how he started with just a shovel and one pick-up, and I remember how I helped him set up his landscaping business. Today, he has a massive organization. Somewhere along the way, his partner came in and they decided to get into the poolside business as well. As it turns out, the partner has the poolside business license. With him pulling out, it is a

bit of a struggle to go through. However, with this move comes a lot of freedom for him.

Despite him being my mentor, he is always open to hear stuff from me. Even mentors need someone that they can discuss things with and take ideas from. No one in perfect and everyone is a student for life.

I explained to him how he now had all the time he needed to make things work for him. Yes, it may take him a couple of years, but in the next five years, he would go on to own 100% of the pool business for himself. He wouldn't need a partner or need to rely on others for the licenses. He just needs to hang in there.

For me, John is someone I really look up to. I had seen him sleeping on the couch when he didn't have anything, and I see him today leading a life most can only dream of. He is someone that has always spoken the truth, regardless of the impact it might have. While he and his former partner continue to be good friends, it is only their business relationship that came to an end.

I have had legitimately toxic workers that really, really got on my nerves and messed things up. Normally, if I am cutting someone off, I always feel bad about it. For some insanely toxic workers, I didn't. However, things get much worse when you are trying to say goodbye to someone that you care about.

LEAD, SERVE, WIN.

You know them, you know that they are trying to deliver their best, but the details just don't seem to add up. While you try your best to highlight their weaknesses and hope that they would be able to cope up, you might be in for a very tough one. Letting them know that they are not mixing well or able to produce the kind of results you need, that's always going to be hard. However, what must be done, must be done – Be truthful.

The problem is that if you do not speak the truth and let such people know what the problem is, it is going to be a trial by fire for you, a death by a thousand cuts. Slowly and gradually, this person will cause more losses in the long run, and that is something you can put an end to before any of it begins. All you need to do is to speak the truth and let them know how it isn't working out between the two of you.

The longer you delay, the lesser of yourself you will become. Your principles will continue to deteriorate, and to make matters worse, others may actually notice that. This would imply that they too can get away with a few mistakes. Do you see? The entire set of principles you set for yourself and for the firm, all of it just starts to unravel only because you can't find it soon enough to speak the truth.

Truth Sets You Free

Not everyone is a fan of speaking the truth, which is why most people would rush in to make up things as they go. The only problem is that such an approach doesn't last long. Not only does it go on to affect your trustworthiness, but it also has a massive impact on any business you may be doing. The beauty, on the other hand, is that if you speak truth to power, you may occasionally be wrong, and that okays. Why? Because it would attract someone with the right kind of power to come in and correct you.

"Isn't that going to embarrass you?"

Not really. If anything, that allows you to learn more. If you had shared something that isn't correct, someone will jump in to ensure you know the facts right. As a result, you walk away from the conversation a more learned person. What's the harm in that?

Take a look at John. On quite a few occasions, I have told him things that I thought and he would come back and correct me where I went wrong.

Moving to Florida

I remember how I brought the discussion up with John about me thinking to move to Florida. John listened to me intently and waited until I was done.

"Tim. You have a corporate job here, and you have a lot of stuff going on here. Why would you want to move to Florida then?"

I gave him my X, Y, and Z reasons.
"Okay, great! However, would you moving to Florida help you resolve these problems?"
"No. Actually, it doesn't."

It took me two years from this point in order to move to Florida. Why? Because John heard me and my truth. Instead of criticizing me, he corrected me and showed me that my impulsive decision was not one that would benefit me. It made sense. I stood corrected, and the following two years allowed me to fill up all the gaps, such as arranging money to buy a house in Florida, taking care of the business, and so on. Now, I have a house that is in my name. I am living comfortably here and this could have gone very wrong had I been impulsive back then. I listened to reason and it made sense.

Say It or Face It

Speaking Truth to power is more like a muscle. The more you work it up, the stronger it becomes.

I started the Parents of High Achieving Students Podcast to promote education products from Mark Cuban and Shaan Patel. When you find yourself in a situation where people are way more successful than you and are part of the decision-making process, you know that there is some kind of power involved.

If you're the smartest person in the room, you're probably in the wrong room, but if you're the least influential, it's hard to make your voice heard. I have nothing but respect and gratitude for Mark and Shaan, but even the greatest of men have blind spots.

I was confident that our team had everything we needed to launch a successful podcast with some research and hard work, but someone in the room who wrote a book about the power of outsourcing insisted that we bring in a friend of his friend who had a podcast creation business. The fact that he told me I shouldn't do any research before talking to his connection. Always be suspicious when somebody tells you not to do any research.

"We don't understand podcasting the way he does."

LEAD, SERVE, WIN.

Anyone who discourages me from doing my due diligence immediately leaves my circle of trust. Despite my objections, everyone seemed on board with bringing on this consultant, so I reluctantly agreed to work with him. Since then, I regretted every moment. Things got ugly and messy. I didn't regret us working with him; I regretted the fact that I didn't take a stand and speak truth to the powers that were present. I should have had the courage to continue speaking my mind, but fear took over. This was a great opportunity, and I wanted the green light enough to make major compromises on the vision.

While I had some great interviews on that podcast, and made some great friendships with some of my guests, I spent more time fighting the people who were supposed to help me. I caught them in outright lies, and they never delivered on the results they promised. Eventually the team agreed to cancel the contract, but the momentum was gone. The team's enthusiasm for the podcast was gone, and so was mine. Instead I switched gears to focus on my own creative projects – like this book - which despite not having the backing of Shark Tank billionaires don't suffer from having too many chefs in the kitchen.

The Takeaway

Speaking truth to power requires you to have courage and guts. While it may seem easy, it can often be extremely challenging, especially when there are others involved who have a greater say in things. Regardless, there are one of two ways you can go about it:

1. You can cave in and regret every moment later on
2. You can speak your mind and stand your ground

Of course, the latter is easier said than done, but it is something that shows your character, grit, and resilience. Yes, you may have to break away from some deals or opportunities, but it is better to remain true to yourself as opposed to seeking something that isn't in alignment with your goal. If you do that, you would end up becoming someone you aren't, and your goals would be far away from your reach.

Write: Is there someone you're afraid to confront? Why?

Chapter 10

Believe In Yourself – Know Your Weaknesses

Whether you are trying to build a business from the ground-up or you are aiming to put together a team, the first thing you need to do is to believe in yourself and your vision.

This might sound cliched by now but the fact remains that if you do not believe in yourself, it shows. When your team or your clients are able to see that you don't really believe in yourself, they would know you don't really believe in what you stand for. As a result, they would leave and choose someone else to work with.

It makes perfect sense, doesn't it? How can you ask your team to believe if you, of all the people, refuse to believe in yourself? It's not possible.

Set a Deadline

Setting a deadline allows you to create a time-constrained goal. Having a goal in life and never really knowing by when are you aiming to achieve it is another form of lying to yourself. Every day, you would feel like you have all the time to get started at a later date. This would continue on and on until the goal fades away or you are just too late to even begin.

For most people, a one to two-year plan should be fine. While it is okay to have a 5-year plan, the fact is that most people would end up quitting at some point. This is because 5 years is a very long time. You never know what might change down the road just after the first year.

I know what you're thinking – How is any of this related to believing in yourself and knowing your weaknesses – bear with me on this one.

I know what I need to achieve in my life and to ensure I get started, I put a deadline for myself that I will quit my corporate job by the end of this year. It was just a few weeks ago that I decided that, but I now stand firm on my decision because I believe in myself. I know that I am capable of doing whatever I set my mind to. There is no goal big enough, no vision too unachievable that I can't pursue and accomplish. All I need is to believe that I can.

Don't get me wrong; the money is good at my job. However, with time, I felt like I was getting a bit too comfortable. If I become too comfortable and too dependent, I would never leave my job. There would always be another reason for me to stick around "Just one more week." Now, none of that matters to me anymore. All that matters is that I believe in myself and that I will pursue a better life for myself. To do that, I will quit my job and start afresh from 2023.

People don't really know what freedom tastes like if they have always been a part of the corporate world. Think about it; 10 years I had my own company. This very company allowed me to travel the world, start school in places I could have never even imagined, and it allowed me to live however I wanted to. That is the kind of experience no corporate job can offer, and that is freedom that I crave for.

When 2020 hit, I took the safe move and joined the corporate side of things. I am not saying that I regret the decision – I own it – but I did get to see the other side of the coin.

If you are an entrepreneur, joining a corporate organization is the last thing you would want to do. To begin with, there are far too many people involved and all of them are constantly trying to clip your wings. You can't do what you know is right; you do what you are told. Whether that suits you well or goes against what you stand for, you must do it, and an entrepreneur is one that simply cannot allow that to happen.

The amount of efforts you put in a corporate sector, all of it is rewarded by 5% or may be 10% raise in your compensation. Ask yourself; is that justifiable? If you were to put in the same amount of efforts in your own business, you would be increasing your payout exponentially.

Having seen both the sides, what I am doing is taking an educated and calculated risk. I have seen both these sides which puts me in the perfect spot to decide which one is better. There are many who have never seen or experienced a corporate job as well as those who have never been entrepreneurs. Those who have been both are lucky enough to work out the difference. Naturally, you would always choose to be an entrepreneur any given day. It's not easy at all, but it is far more rewarding than any corporate job on the planet.

For most people, freedom seems a touch too fictitious. However, for someone like me, it was an easy decision. I am wired in a particularly way, which is probably why I choose to go back. You may be wired a bit differently, and that is okay too.

If everyone was to be an entrepreneur, the world would be in a chaotic state right now. We wouldn't have gardeners, mechanics, doctors, lawyers, politicians, and that would have upset the balance. It is not up to me to dictate you to walk my path. If that isn't you, it's okay. However, if you are someone that thinks in those terms, start off by setting yourself a deadline.

"Okay. By this end of this year/next year, I would quit my job and pursue my entrepreneurial journey."

You need to have a deadline because it is by doing so that you actually take timely actions. You start acting more responsibly. You start ensuring that you are tackling all the things that need to be handled, such as paying bills, providing to your house, paying your taxes, et cetera.

It must be a well though-out plan in order for you to go out there and do something different. The better laid out your plan is, the easier it will be for you to stick with it. The only other option is slavery, or at least that's how I look at jobs.

I can't imagine living my life, depending on the 9 to 5 job that earns me a paycheck. To me, that amount is the amount is sold all my dreams for. My dreams are far more valuable than any amount written on those checks, and I cannot sell those off.

Everyone is entitled to their own views and values. There are those who would support my move and then there would be those who would oppose it. It's all okay! Your plan won't be affected. For you, all that would matter is to ensure you check all the boxes, get stuff done and move closer to achieving all the tasks within the plan.

For me, this book is an integral piece for my master plan. It was a part of the plan I had designed for myself. I had already set a deadline that this book must be done and out by the end of 2022 – Well, here it is!

When you set goals with an expiration date, you find courage and determination to go out there and get stuff done. These won't be goals that would be hung up on the board gathering dust. The more you see them, the more you would want to strike them off.

"Okay. So, I have to do this and that in the next two weeks. Let's figure out how."

From there, you start moving, even though it may be the wrong direction, but you are moving nonetheless. It is progress, and any progress beats perfection any given day.

"Difficult to see; always in motion is the future."

Yoda, The Empire Strikes Back

Yoda puts it in perfect words. Your plans are only as good as the actions you take towards the plan. I can plan on to be a millionaire in 2 years. Great. I might even have the best plan of all in place. Fantastic. However, for the next 2 years, I just sit and wait to become a millionaire because my plan says I will. Pfft! That's never going to happen.

You work towards something if you believe that you have the ability to do it. If you only plan and never really take action, it shows that you don't think it is possible. You aren't really be truthful to yourself and your plan.

For me, this book had to be done in a timely manner because if it wasn't the case, I wouldn't be able to do the other things that are lined up. It would start piling up and it would all lead to a disaster.

It's Okay to Make Mistakes

They say progress is better than perfection. You can lie in your bed, waiting for that perfect opportunity to arrive that you can grab and become a millionaire, or you can get up and create the opportunity yourself. The first one, I assure you, won't do you any good. The second one, I also assure you, would fetch you results. They may be riddled with mistakes and errors, but it would be far better than the "perfect" scenario you had in your mind. At least, you would have ended somewhere other than your bed.

When we set goals, we break them down into milestones. This is a great way for us to keep track of our progress. At no point in time do we expect the perfect results. They are always above or below what we might expect, and that's just how things work. At any given moment in time, we would know exactly where we stand and what's to come next. That's how you plan, make mistakes, revisit your plan and revise. With time, the plan becomes better and better and you continue to do more and more things. After each milestone, you continue to take action towards the next goal. Not long after, you just need to look back and realize just how far you have come from where you started, and that is a very rewarding feeling.

What Happens If You Don't Believe?

Jordan Peterson once said:

If you think strong men are dangerous, wait till you see what weak men are capable of!

The fact is that you don't believe in yourself, you become a weaker person. There won't be much in life that you would be able to accomplish.

I have been a part of the fitness circle for quite a while now. When it comes to genetic potential, a lot of people quickly tune into a video or two on YouTube to see if they have what it takes to build a good body shape. Most of them would immediately pull away because they would believe they can't. Wrong! You never really know until you try bodybuilding. You can't really have the faintest of ideas just how capable you are because you are not believing in the idea that you can do something if you want. Instead, you choose to believe in a video that may or may not have stated some facts.

There are so many people out there who could have never built their bodies the way they did had YouTube existed back then. People like Arnold, Stallone, and many others defied the odds and ended up with bodies that have gone down in the history books. Why? They believed in themselves and they finally achieved the results.

You can't really make a body in just a matter of months. It takes three consistent years of training in order for you to finally create the kind of body you have wanted. It literally does not matter what you look like right now. All you need is to believe that you have what it takes to change that and give it your best for the next three years. Trust me, do that and you would be thanking me later. While you may not have any idea of how you would look like after three years, you can count on the fact that you would look 100% better than you do right now if you remain consistent.

When you don't believe in yourself, you don't move towards a goal. If you don't move towards a goal, you won't make any progress. This applies to both the entrepreneurs and those who are working a day-time job.

A lot of people dream of meeting people like Grant Cardone, but what they don't really realize is that they can. You need to prove your mettle and you need to take actions if you really want to meet people like him or be in the same room as him. I have because I worked towards that goal. I believed that I can make it happen; Lo and behold, I made it.

The Takeaway

Believe! Believe that you can, and you will. Believe that you can achieve your goals, work towards those goals, and you will. You can never really work towards anything if you don't believe you have what it takes.

I've been working on this – my first book - for years, and as I finalize these last few chapters, I'm already thinking about the chapters for my second and third books. This may not be the perfect book, but completing it feels like a miracle. Here's how I did it:

1. Set goals you believe you can accomplish.
2. Write a deadline you believe you can stick to.
3. Work your butt off to get it done.
4. Win!

Write: Set a goal with a deadline.

Chapter 11

Support Your Team's Side Hustle

Jon T. Banning and JTB Landscapers were big parts of my time in Las Vegas. I helped Jon build marketing workflows and a team to carry out the plan. Jon started with just a shovel and an old Chevy, and now he's on billboards all over the Las Vegas Strip and provides jobs that support dozens upon dozens of families, and I'm honored to have helped him build that. However, there came a time when I knew that I had accomplished my primary mission with Jon's company, and that I was being called to work more intensively with kids. Not only did Jon support my vision with the same enthusiasm that I supported his, he actually hired me to tutor his two daughters. Jon modeled the principle that I'm about to teach you.

In the early days of Tim's Tutors, I had hired some experienced educators. The problem was that most of them thought they were the best and knew better than anyone on how to do the job. There was a clear clash of vision. I was capitalizing on the failures of the education system – Las Vegas had the highest dropout rate in the country – and there were people on my team who had bought into that failing system.

With time, I realized that regardless of age or experience, I needed to hire people who were more teachable. Every person comes with their own unique dreams and goals. While they would have nothing to do with mine or yours, it is good to know that they had something they were aiming for.

Once, I hired a college sophomore named Zoie who wanted to be a fashion designer and she was actually good in teaching a few subjects. Furthermore, she was really solid on social media, something I had been handling solo in the beginning.

I told her, "I know that your goal isn't to be a lifelong educator, and that's okay. However, I know that you are a way better designer than I am. You are way better at all this artistic stuff. Here's a video I made. Edit the daylights out of it and remove what you think is useless." She did a much better job than I would have at the video editing. In fact, she earned my trust to the point where I gave her an actual fashion design project: creating company uniforms for the team.

It was my idea to always have a weekly check in with my people to see what they were doing. Part of my goal was to ensure I appreciated everyone who were doing good or who had other talents that I knew of. Giving the video to her allowed me to test her skills and allowed her to show just what she can do. Despite the fact that I knew she wouldn't stick around forever, I still wanted to give her something to work on that was in line with her goals. In fact, I was impressed by her work and I decided to let her use my connections to see if she could land a better opportunity for herself. It didn't seem like a wise business move, but it allowed her to scratch that itch to create while serving my greater vision.

I allowed her to shout herself out on the social media so that she could be noticed more by the people that were already within my circle. She had legitimately designed the uniforms, so there was a relevant connection to her passion in every photo in which we wore those uniforms. I wanted her to find a platform upon which she could create her presence and use it to propel her own line of work. In the end, she got to put our company uniforms on her portfolio and resume, allowing her to showcase that at the next available opening. I got a budding designer who gave me free advertising every time she looked for work, and more importantly, a smooth transition for all my clients she was responsible for when it was time for her to move on.

She did a fantastic job and I had supported her as much as I could. I wanted her to grow while she was with us so that when she chose to part ways, she would have already gathered enough steam and momentum to carry her forward. When you help people accomplish their dreams or even move closer to them, you are creating perpetual ripples that will resonate with them for the rest of their lives.

"Be of service to the many, for service to the many leads to greatness!"

Jim Rohn

When you help others, you draw in the right people. They won't be looking to make money off you; they would just want to be there with you. Helping someone go to the next level allows you to be helped by God in His own mysterious ways.

I know I have written numerous recommendation letters, and I have tried to be as generous as possible. Why should I write something that would end up hurting their chances at finding better opportunities or gaining success?

If you have some kind of power that can allow you to help someone; help them. Do not back off because you aren't going to retain these people for life. You might, but why take the chance? They may forget what you said, but they will always remember how you made them feel, and that's something I have heard and seen time and again.

Think about it; if you are helping people, it's just good word-of-mouth for you and your firm. People will come to know of you one way or another and the right people will start coming towards you, whether as clients or as candidates. That's what you need, and that's how you create a legacy for yourself.

"Tim – He helped everyone he could!"

Here's another thing. If your people aren't making enough at your place and need a second job, you don't really have any reason why you should advise them on what to do. Secondly, if someone doesn't have a passion for something but you are somewhat forcing them to do it, you're only going to create hard resentment. I have seen people doing this without realizing the effects it will have at their firm later on.

The Takeaway

A leader is one that inspires others to go after what they wish to pursue. A leader is one that inspires them to do things they thought they couldn't. If you stop supporting your people, you're just making them do a job and you are just doing yours as well. You stop being a leader and start being a boss that is hated and loathed by others. The only reason they would work for you is for that paycheck at the end of the month. There will be no motivation for them other than their income at the end of the month. This means that whatever happens between those 30 days, they would only do enough to make it look acceptable. In such an environment, don't expect anyone to think outside of the box or do something beyond the ordinary. Your firm, all of a sudden, will become ordinary, and why would anyone want to do business with a firm that's just okay to begin with? Makes sense, doesn't it?

Write: Is there someone on my team that has a side project I can support?

Chapter 12

Let Your Yes Be Yes – Let Your No Be No

Sometimes, you just need to trust your instincts. Sometimes, just let your gut guide you.

When I started the Parents of High Achieving Students Podcast. A friend of a friend of someone close to Mark Cuban brought in somebody from his "good old boys network" to provide help for the podcast that we never needed or asked for. My gut screamed no, and I made my position clear many times, but office politics ruled the day, and I grudgingly agreed to "try him out." It was my gut instinct that turned and twisted and made me feel like this wasn't the right move. Eventually, I was proven right in the worst way. This consultant derailed the podcast to the point where all the buy-in for creating it in the first place was gone. Never agree to try something or someone out that should have been a hard no from the start.

When I used to prepare my students for the SAT, I would tell them to trust their gut. There is no point in going back at the end of the section and check all your answers in the last three or four minutes. You are only going to end up confusing yourself if you do that. Why? Your mind will start pacing and it would cloud your judgement. Now that you won't be thinking clearly, you might end up changing some of the answers that were perfectly fine at first, but with these changes, they now stand as incorrect. As a result, you would lose marks and that would hurt your overall SAT scores.

Sometimes, you just have to stick to your guns!

"I've seen what such feelings can do to a fully trained Jedi Knight. To the best of us."

Ahsoka Tano, The Mandalorian

When you are working your formulas and questions, you know what you are doing. However, in those last few minutes, it is not some light-bulb that goes off that pushes you to change your answers, it is fear – A feeling. Feelings can greatly get in the way of logic, and the SAT is a test designed to test your logic and aptitude, not your emotions. It is a bad practice and a bad idea to revisit your answers.

Learn How to Say No as Well

Yes must always be yes. However, you can't expect to say yes to everything. If someone comes up to you and asks you to kick a puppy or punch a kitten, would you do it? No. Definitely not! Instead, if you end up saying yes because the guy was "really adamant" or someone you "just can't say no to," well… you are a terrible person. You would have no one else to blame but yourself for not listening to your gut instincts and not saying "No" when it really mattered.

As leaders, we are supposed to know when to say yes and when to say no. The difference between a leader and a boss is that a boss would always say no to pretty much everything whereas a leader would only say no to something that would affect them, the company, or the person on the other end of the table. A leader will always try and find a way to make things better, not worst.

"I am sorry to hear about your loss. Take your time and be with the family." This is a more human approach. A typical corporate boss would say something like this:

"I am sorry to hear about your loss. You can come in late today." WHAT? A person just experienced a loss and you still expect them to come in for the day? That's just wrong (not the word I am thinking of).

If I was on the other end, I know I would have said "no" and would have walked away from such a toxic environment. These little things really matter, and there is no reason why you can't say no to something you find wrong.

Learning how to say no allows you to set healthy boundaries as well. While this may cause you to create some friction in the workplace, the fact is that no one would ever try and cross that boundary because you would have made it absolutely clear.

Gut is always faster than the mind!

If you learn and practice using your guts, you will end up eliminating a lot of doubts that find their way in your head. You may have learned how to avoid listening to your gut instincts, but it is time to learn how to use it instead.

Trust, But Verify

Being a leader or an entrepreneur, you are more than likely going to trust your team. That's actually a good thing. However, remember, we are all a bunch of human beings living with our own core values. Some of us may have really strong moral compasses but others may not. Therefore, while

LEAD, SERVE, WIN.

you can trust your team to get the job done, it is always a good idea to verify that it is done the way you had instructed.

People may think, "Wait, isn't that just a fancy way of saying don't trust others?" That really isn't. I trust Mr. A to do his job, and I know he will. However, I will still verify that everything was done accordingly. He might have missed a few steps or ended up with the wrong results. Either way, by verifying what happened, I would know where he might have gone wrong and then I could jump in to train Mr. A so that the same error does not repeat again.

Sometimes, you just need to go back and make sure. However, the more you do that, the better your gut feeling becomes. Just like I said earlier, your gut is like a muscle that you can work on and grow to perform better. It is designed to help you get results and know if something adds up or if something seems off.

Trust, but verify – Always verify. It doesn't take you hours or weeks or months to do that. It is just a 10-to-20-minute process and you should know exactly what is going on. The more you do so, the better the results for everyone.

Keep Your Word

Part of the lesson comes in the shape of gaining the ability to stick to your words. If you have said yes, you abide by it. If you have said no, make sure it remains a no for that particular thing.

If you don't stand for something, you will fall for anything!

Individuals who do not have any boundaries, they are always pushed around. If you want to be a leader, you need to develop conviction. You need to know what you can say yes to and what you must say no to. No matter what comes, you must always stand up for what you believe in. You shouldn't be someone that can be pushed around because if you are, you aren't truly a leader.

When you are a person who is leading a team or a group of people, you are expected to stay true to your words. This is something with can see with many politicians. They claim they would do this and that, and paint a rose-like picture of a future that sounds great. However, I am yet to come across that future. Ask yourself then; how can you trust them? What happens to someone if they cannot keep their words and bend to pressure? Simple – They lose popularity and lose their followers.

People who stick by their words are people who others look up to. These are the people that set examples and lead others. They are the people that are worthy to be followed to the end of the worlds if needed. This is because they know what they need to do, what they stand for, and what they aim for.

This also goes well for those who are decision makers. If you make a decision, that's it. Always stick with your decision regardless of the outcome. You would end up with some results either way. You would either learn that the decision wasn't as productive, and come back strong, or you would find success and know "Okay, this works!"

If you allow others to sway you consistently, you are letting everyone know that you are never in control of your life. You are letting others know that you cannot stick by your words and that anyone can easily manipulate you to alter your course in the middle of something. As a result, people would not follow you, would not do business with you, and they would not trust you with their business.

We entrepreneurs are meant to be decision-makers. We are supposed to make those hard choices that most aren't ready to make. We must thrive on learning and the best way to learn is to make a decision and be open to lessons that you pick up along the way.

I know that many of you may not be happy making mistakes, but failure, as it turns out, is the greatest teacher of them all. Through failure, you can learn a lot more and come back even stronger. However, it's one thing to learn from failure, but it is another thing to continue changing your path every single time you fail. That's not what we are aiming for.

TIM PRUNYI

If you want to go to Houston, Texas and on your way, you come across Vegas, you don't say, "Okay, I now want to go to Washington instead." You know your goal, you figure out where you went wrong, correct your heading and go for it. That's how you learn. It is a natural process and it works best when you stick with a plan of action through thick and thin until that plan is either fully discovered or realized.

You have the ability to bring your vision to life because you have the ability to create. We are all made in the likeness of God, and that means we have this innate ability to create the reality we pursue. However, this power comes to those who stand up for something, who say "yes" where they must, say "no" where they must, and are never swayed by others.

Now you know – Go out there and create!

Write: What am I willing to say yes to and follow through on?

LEAD, SERVE, WIN.

Conclusion

Being an entrepreneur is a dream that comes with a price. It takes grit, commitment, and above all, it takes nerves to help you go through some challenging times.
I owned a business that survived for over a decade. Only about three percent of businesses ever make it that far. I was a three per enter. Then, I gave in to fear, and surrendered my freedom to join the corporate world. I could blame it on the lockdowns and shutdowns – which were legitimately devastating – or I could look within to see why I doubted myself in the first place. Today, I know where I am going back because I experienced both sides and I know what I really want. Regardless of the outcome, I will have faith in myself and the God who made me.

The point of writing this book was not to intimidate you or scare you; it was to highlight some of the things I learned, some of the challenges I faced, and to teach you what you can expect moving forwards in life.

You may have your own unique sets of values, and I respect that. However, if you truly wish to step into the world of entrepreneurship, you need to find that courage within you to stand up for what you believe in. You need to learn how to manage and lead others. You need to learn how to bring in that human element as opposed to a software making your decisions for you.

Being an entrepreneur is far more rewarding than any corporate job, at least for me. While it takes time to find those rewards and acquire said freedom, I know I will happily go through that because I know I can. If I doubted my skills or myself, I would have never even thought about setting a goal to quit my corporate job by the end of this year. Most likely, by the time you would be reading this, I would have made that move. If not, you can always follow me on my social media to find out more.

My journey is one that begins all over again. You don't have to wait that long though. Learn from my lessons, learn from my errors, and apply those to your life. Make your journey a memorable one. I hope that this book did help you and gave you some good nuggets. I am hoping to hear more about your success one day. Until then, *never stop leading. Never stop serving. Never stop winning!*

Made in the USA
Columbia, SC
27 November 2022